10 Minute Guide to
Quattro Pro® 3

10 Minute Guide to Quattro Pro® 3

SAMS

A Division of Macmillan Computer Publishing
11711 North College, Carmel, Indiana 46032 USA

International Standard Book Number: 0-672-30122-9
Library of Congress Catalog Card Number: 90-61698

Publisher: *Richard K. Swadley*
Publishing Manager: *Marie Butler-Knight*
Managing Editor: *Majorie Hopper*
Acquisitions Editor: *Stephen R. Poland*
Development Editor: *Lisa Bucki*
Technical Editor: *Tracy Kaufman*
Manuscript Editor: *Ronda Carter Henry*
Editorial Assistant: *Tracy Kaufman*
Cover Designer: *Dan Armstrong*
Indexer: *Sue VandeWalle*
Production Team: *Brad Chinn, Denny Hager, Sarah Leatherman, Johnna VanHoose*

Printed in the United States of America

Trademarks

All terms mentioned in this book that are known to be trademarks or service marks are listed below. In addition, terms suspected of being trademarks or service marks have been appropriately capitalized. SAMS cannot attest to the accuracy of this information. Use of a term in this book should not be regarded as affecting the validity of any trademark or service mark.

Quattro Pro 3.0 is a registered trademark of Borland International, Inc.

MS-DOS is a registered trademark of Microsoft Corporation.

All other product and service names are trademarks and service marks of their respective owners.

Contents

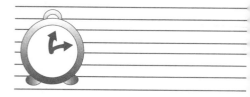

Introduction

Perhaps you walked into work this morning and found that Quattro Pro 3 had been installed on your computer. There was a note stuck to your monitor that said, "We need a report to present at Friday's meeting. See what you can do." Now what? A few things are certain:

• You need to learn the program quickly.

• You need to identify and learn only the tasks necessary to accomplish your goal.

• You need a clear, step-by-step way to learn about the basic features of the program.

Welcome to the *10 Minute Guide to Quattro Pro 3*.

Because most people are pressed for time and need to be able to begin using new software programs quickly, the *10 Minute Guide* leads the reader through the most important features of the program in a simple, no-fluff format.

Most people don't have the luxury of sitting down uninterrupted for hours at a time to learn a new program, so the *10 Minute Guide* teaches you the operations you need in lessons that can be completed in 10 minutes or less. Not

1

only does the 10 minute format offer information in bite-sized, easy to follow modules (making operations easy to learn and retain), it allows you to stop and start as often as you like because each lesson is a self-contained series of steps related to a particular task.

What Are the 10 Minute Guides?

The *10 Minute Guide* is a new approach to learning computer programs. Instead of trying to teach everything about a particular software product, the *10 Minute Guides* teach you only about the most often-used features in a particular program. Organized in lesson format, each *10 Minute Guide* contains between 20 and 30 short lessons.

You will find only simple English used to explain the procedures in this book. With straightforward procedures, easy-to-follow steps, and special artwork (called icons), the *10 Minute Guides* make learning a new software program easy and fast.

The following icons help you find your way around in the *10 Minute Guide to Quattro Pro 3*:

Timesaver Tips offer shortcuts and hints for using the program effectively.

Plain English icons appear when new terms are defined.

Panic Button icons appear where new users often run into trouble.

A Table of Features and a Table of Functions are included at the end of the book, providing you with a quick guide to Quattro Pro features that are not given full coverage in this book. You can use this table either as a reference for more information or as a quick guide to finding the keystrokes you need in order to perform routine operations.

Specific conventions are used to help you find your way around Quattro Pro as easily as possible:

What You Type
: Within the numbered steps, the information you type is printed in a second color

Menu Names
: The names of Quattro Pro menus are displayed with the first letter capitalized

Also, after Lesson 2, the word *select* will be used to tell you when to use the mouse or keyboard to highlight a menu name, option, cell block, etc.

Who Should Use the *10 Minute Guide to Quattro Pro 3*?

The *10 Minute Guide to Quattro Pro 3* is the answer for anyone who

- Needs to learn Quattro Pro quickly.

- Feels overwhelmed by the complexity of the Quattro Pro program.

- Is a new computer user and is intimidated by learning new programs.

3

- Wants a clear, concise guide to the most important features of the Quattro Pro program.

Whether you are a manager, a member of an office support staff, a lawyer, a doctor, a teacher, an entrepreneur, or simply a computer novice, the *10 Minute Guide to Quattro Pro 3* will help you find and learn the most important aspects of the Quattro Pro program as quickly as possible.

What Is In This Book?

The *10 Minute Guide to Quattro Pro 3* is organized in a series of lessons, ranging from basic start up to a few more advanced features. Remember that nothing in this book is difficult. Although most users will want to start at the beginning of the book and progress through the lessons sequentially, you can follow the lessons in any order.

If Quattro Pro has not been installed on your computer, consult the inside front cover for installation steps. If you need to review basic DOS commands to prepare disks, see the DOS Primer in the back of this book.

For Further Reference, Consult. . .

The First Book of Quattro Pro, Revised Edition, from SAMS

Quattro Pro In Business, from SAMS

Lessons

Lesson 1
Starting and Exiting Quattro Pro

In this lesson you'll learn how to start and exit, change screen display modes, and get help in Quattro Pro 3.0.

Starting Quattro Pro

You can only run Quattro Pro if your computer has a hard disk drive. To start Quattro Pro, follow these steps:

1. Change to the directory that contains your Quattro Pro program files (for example, type `CD\QPRO` and press Enter).

2. Type the letter `Q` and press Enter.

   Start-Up Blues If you need to review basic DOS procedures for starting your computer, answering the date and time prompts, and changing directories, consult the DOS Primer in the back of this book.

After Quattro Pro's opening screen, the worksheet screen shown in Figure 1-1 appears.

When your computer is equipped with a mouse, Quattro Pro automatically detects the mouse type and adjusts itself accordingly. The far left button on the mouse is the active button, which can be used with Quattro Pro's *Mouse*

Palette. Figure 1-1 shows the Mouse Palette on the right side of the screen (if you don't have a mouse, the Mouse Palette will not be visible).

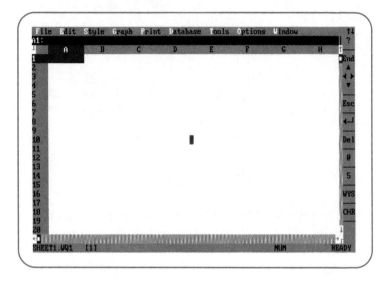

Figure 1-1. *The Quattro Pro worksheet screen.*

Changing the Screen Mode

When you installed Quattro Pro 3.0, you chose whether to display the screen in *WYSIWYG* or character mode. For machines with less power, Quattro Pro runs faster in character mode.

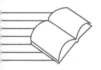

WYSIWYG WYSIWYG is the acronym for What You See Is What You Get. WYSIWYG mode enables you to display your work on-screen as it will look when it is printed.

To change the screen display mode, follow these steps:

6

1. Press the / (forward slash) to activate the Menu bar and press O. Or click on Options in the Menu bar (if you are unfamiliar with mouse terminology or how to use the mouse, refer to Lesson 2). The Options pull-down menu, shown in Figure 1-2, appears.

2. Select the Hardware option by pressing H and Enter with the keyboard or by clicking on Hardware with the mouse. Quattro Pro displays the Hardware submenu.

3. Select the Display mode option by pressing D and Enter or by clicking on Display mode.

4. Quattro Pro displays a list of possible screen modes. Select the mode you want and press Enter.

In the above steps, the term *pull-down menu* was used. For more information on how to use pull-down menus, refer to Lesson 3.

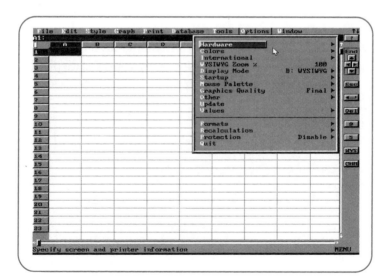

Figure 1-2. The Options pull-down menu.

7

Quattro Pro returns to the worksheet screen in the new display mode.

How to Run Faster Choice B: WYSIWYG mode runs slower because the graphics are better. The alternative choices offer faster modes but less graphic displays. For example, if your computer has an EGA monitor, select option C:EGA 80X43.

Getting Help

Quattro Pro's Help screens are *context-sensitive,* which means that at any time you can get help on the subject you are currently working on. For example, if you are building a graph, you can easily open the Graphs help screen. In Figure 1-3, the Help screen has been accessed from a blank worksheet. The following steps explain how to use the help feature:

1. Press F1. The Quattro Pro Help Index screen appears, as shown in Figure 1-3. A list of help topics is displayed, followed by a brief description.

2. Select Help and press Enter. The Using the Quattro Pro Help System screen appears, as shown in Figure 1-4.

3. Press Esc to close the Help screen.

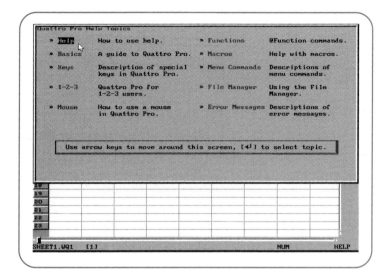

Figure 1-3. *The Help Index screen.*

Figure 1-4. *The Using the Quattro Pro Help System screen.*

Exiting Quattro Pro

To exit Quattro Pro and return to DOS after finishing a work session, follow these steps:

1. Press the / (forward slash) to activate the Menu bar, type F and press Enter. Or click on File in the Menu bar. The File pull-down menu shown in Figure 1-5 appears.

2. Press X and Enter to select Exit with the keyboard or click on Exit with the mouse. Notice that the accelerator key for exiting Quattro Pro is not E, but *X*.

3. If you have made changes to the worksheet without saving them, Quattro Pro displays a *dialog box* asking you if you wish to save the worksheet with the changes. Lesson 6 explains how to name and save a worksheet.

Exiting Quickly The speed key combination for exiting Quattro Pro is Ctrl+X.

Dialog Box A dialog box is a box that appears on-screen that conveys or requests more information to perform an operation.

The term *accelerator key* was used in the above steps. To find out more information about accelerator keys, refer to Lesson 3.

In this lesson you learned how to start and exit, change the screen display mode, and get help in Quattro Pro. In the next lesson you will learn how to navigate the Quattro Pro worksheet.

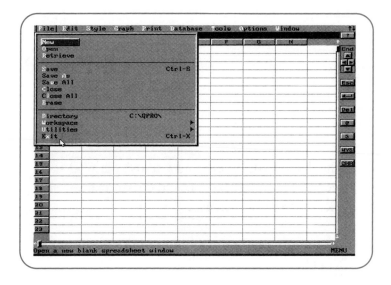

Figure 1-5. *The File pull-down menu.*

Lesson 2
Moving Around the Worksheet

In this lesson you'll learn how to use the worksheet screen and move quickly around the worksheet using the keyboard or the mouse.

The Worksheet Screen

A worksheet is divided into cells. Cells are created by the intersection of horizontally numbered rows and vertically alphabetized columns. If you are in WYSIWYG mode, you can see the grid lines that outline the cells. Figure 2-1 shows the screen in WYSIWYG mode with the grid lines displayed.

Following is a list which details the parts of the worksheet screen:

Menu Bar The bar across the top of the screen containing the menu names; each can be pulled-down to reveal commands

Input Line Directly beneath the Menu bar; it displays the cell selector location and when you enter information, it first appears on the Input line

Cell Selector Used to navigate the worksheet; when a worksheet is first opened, the cell selector is in cell A1

Mouse Pointer In WYSIWYG mode, the mouse pointer resembles an arrowhead; in character mode it is a small rectangle

Message Line Located in the bottom left corner of the screen; displays the name of the worksheet, or when a menu is pulled down, a description of the option

Mode Indicator Located in the bottom right corner of the screen; when Quattro Pro is waiting for cell input, the status line reads READY

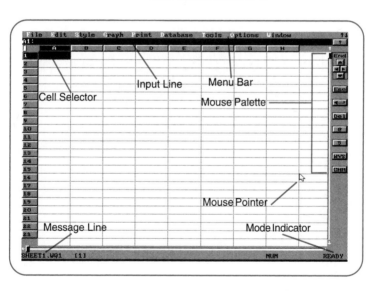

Figure 2-1. The Quattro Pro worksheet screen shown in WYSIWYG mode so that the grid lines are visible.

Moving the Cell Selector with the Keyboard

The appearance of the cell selector varies, depending on the type of monitor you have. If, for example, you have a black and white monitor, the cell selector appears in reverse video. On a color monitor, it appears in a different color. When you open a new worksheet, the cell selector is in cell A1. Table 2-1 explains the keystrokes you use to move the cell selector in Quattro Pro.

Table 2-1. Cursor Movement Keys.

Press	To move
→	Right one cell
←	Left one cell
↓	Down one cell
↑	Up one cell
Tab	Left one screen
Shift-Tab	Right one screen
Home	Cell A1
PgDn	Down one screen
PgUp	Up one screen

Place the cell selector in cell A1 and try the following steps to get a feel for moving the cell selector with the keyboard:

1. Press ↓. The cell selector should now be located in cell A2, and the Input line displays A2.

2. Press ↑ twice. The first time you press the key, the cell selector moves to cell A1. After that, Quattro Pro beeps at you to let you know that you have reached the top of the worksheet.

3. Press PgDn. The cell selector jumps a full screen down. If the screen is displaying in 80×43 character mode, the cell selector moved to cell A21.

4. Press Home. The cell selector jumps back to cell A1.

5. Press Tab. The cell selector jumps a full screen to the right. If your screen is displaying in 80×43 character mode, the cell selector moved to cell I1.

6. Press Home to move the cell selector back to cell A1.

7. Press End and then press ↓. The cell selector immediately jumps to the bottom row of the worksheet, row 8,192.

8. Press End and then press →. The cell selector jumps to the cell furthest from cell A1, cell IV8192.

9. Press Home. The cell selector returns to cell A1.

The portion of the worksheet that you see on-screen at once is quite small compared to the total number of cells—2,097,152! Each worksheet has 256 columns by 8,192 rows. Figure 2-2 gives you a perspective on the screen versus the entire worksheet.

Moving the Cell Selector with the Mouse

If you have not used a mouse before, the following terms are used to describe mouse movements:

Point   Move the mouse pointer to an item on the screen or to a cell.

Click   Rapidly press and release the mouse. button once; if you have more than one button, press the leftmost button.

Drag   Press and hold down the mouse button while you move the mouse pointer.

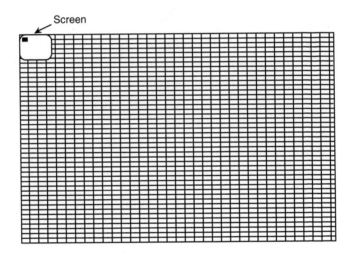

Figure 2-2. The screen in proportion to the total amount of space in the worksheet.

The mouse pointer moves independently. That is, when you move the pointer, the cell selector does not move until you click the mouse button. The cell selector then jumps to the cell or screen item where the mouse pointer is located.

Table 2-2 explains the buttons you can click on in the Mouse Palette. Figure 2-3 shows a close up view of the Mouse Palette.

Table 2-2. The Mouse Palette Icons.

Click on	To
↑	Move the current worksheet from the bottom of the stack of open worksheets to the top.
↓	Move the current worksheet from the top of the stack of open worksheets to the bottom.
End icons (diamond shaped)	Move the cell selector to the four corners of the worksheet when it is blank and to the cells that are on the outside of any entered information.
Esc	Activate Esc.
Return symbol	Activate Enter.
Del	Activate Del.
@	Activate the Quattro Pro formula dialog box.
5	Activate a macro.
WYS	Change the screen display to WYSIWYG mode.
CHR	Change the screen display to character mode.

Another Way to Select Esc or Enter When you enter text in the Input line, [Esc] and [Enter] appear at the far left side of the Input line. You can click on these bracketed commands instead of using the keyboard or the Mouse Palette.

17

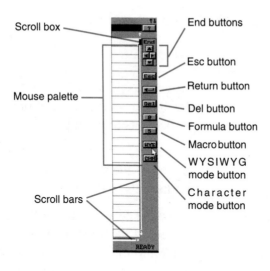

Figure 2-3. The Mouse Palette.

You can also move the cell selector by clicking on the scroll bars. If you drag the little box that is located on the scroll bars, the cell selector moves in the direction you drag. If you simply click on the scroll bar, not on the little box, the cell selector jumps large distances.

Changing the Active Mouse Button

If you are left-handed, you probably want to run the mouse with your left hand. The active mouse button is set for the left button by default. You can change the active mouse button by using the following steps:

1. Click on Options in the Menu Bar.

2. From the Options pull-down menu, click on Hardware.

3. From the Hardware submenu, click on Mouse Button.

4. Click on either the Left or Right option.

5. Click on the Update option in to Options pull-down menu to save your change for the current and all future work sessions.

If you don't select the Update option, the change you made for the mouse button will only be active in the current work session.

For all subsequent lessons, the word *select* will be used to tell you when to use the keyboard or the mouse to highlight a menu name, option, cell block, etc. If you are unsure how to do this, refer back to this lesson.

In this lesson you learned how to move around the worksheet screen with the mouse or keyboard. In the next lesson you will learn how to use Quattro Pro's menus.

Lesson 3
Using Quattro Pro Menus

In this lesson you'll learn how to open the pull-down menus in the Menu bar and select menu options using the keyboard or the mouse.

Quattro Pro Menus

At the top of the worksheet screen is the Menu Bar containing the names of the pull-down menus. In Lesson 1, you opened the Options pull-down menu to change the screen display mode and the File pull-down menu to exit Quattro Pro.

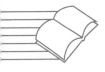

Pull-down Menus The term pull-down menu refers to a menu that remains *hidden* in the Menu bar until you press a key combination or use the mouse to open or *pull down* the menu.

Choosing Menus with the Keyboard

To select the File pull-down menu with the keyboard, follow these steps:

1. Type the / (forward slash) and the letter F (for File). The first letter of each menu name is its *accelerator key.* Typing the accelerator key of a menu after pressing / opens that menu. The File menu is pulled down, as shown in Figure 3-1.

20

2. To close the File menu, press Esc.

Accelerator Keys Accelerator keys (shown in Figure 3-1) are the letters within menu, command, and option names that are displayed in a different color or a brighter format. These keys are used instead of the direction keys to speedily select a menu, command or option. Notice that in many of the submenus, the accelerator keys are not the first letter of the command or option.

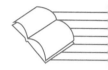

celerator
/s

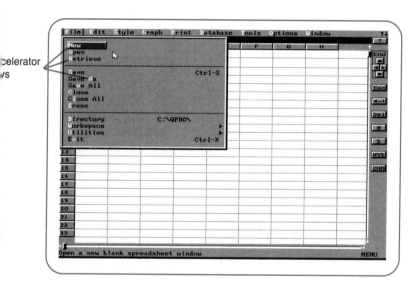

Figure 3-1. The File menu pulled down.

A second way to select a menu is as follows:

1. Press the / (forward slash). The Menu bar is activated, and the cursor is automatically positioned on the File pull-down menu name.

2. Press → 4 times and press Enter. The cursor is moved to and opened the Print pull-down menu, as shown in

21

Figure 3-2. While a pull-down menu is open and you have not selected an option, you can still pull down a different menu by pressing ← or →.

3. Press ← 5 times. Notice that even though the File pull-down menu is furthest to the left, Quattro Pro assumed that you wanted to keep going, and opened the Window pull-down menu.

4. Press Escape to close the Window pull-down menu.

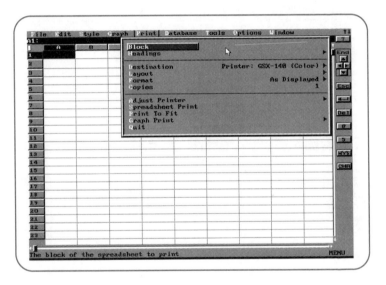

Figure 3-2. The Print menu pulled down.

Choosing Menus with the Mouse

Using the mouse to open a menu is faster and easier than using the keyboard. Use the following steps to select a menu with the mouse:

1. Move the mouse pointer to any menu name in the Menu bar.

2. Click on the menu name. The menu opens and you can select any option on the menu in the same manner.

3. To close the menu press Esc or click anywhere in the worksheet screen outside the menu.

Selecting a Menu Option

After opening a menu, the next step is to select an option from the menu. Use the following steps to display the date and time:

1. Select the Options pull-down menu. Notice that when you opened the Options menu, the cursor was automatically positioned on the first option, Hardware. In the bottom left corner of the screen, a short description of what the selected option does appears. The description for the Hardware option is `Specify screen and printer information`.

2. Press ↓. The cursor moved to the Colors option and the description changed to `Customize screen colors for Quattro Pro`.

3. Move the cursor to each menu option, pausing to read the description of each one. At this point, the descriptions may not mean much but, as you beome more familiar with Quattro Pro, the descriptions become an easy way to remember what each option does.

4. Select the Other option. The Other submenu shown in Figure 3-3 appears. (Note that you cannot pull down a different menu on the Menu bar now that you have selected an option.)

5. Select the Clock option. The Clock submenu appears with several more choices.

6. Select the Standard option. The submenus close.

7. To make the clock selection a permanent feature, select the Update option from the Options pull-down menu.

8. Press Esc. The current date and time should appear at the bottom of your worksheet screen as shown in Figure 3-4.

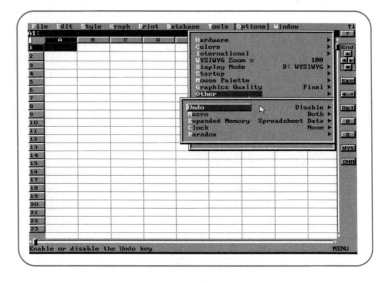

Figure 3-3. *The Options pull-down menu with the Other submenu displayed.*

 **Undisplay the Date and Time** If you prefer not to display the date and time on-screen, remove it by selecting the Options pull-down menu, the Other option, the Clock option and the None option from the Clock submenu.

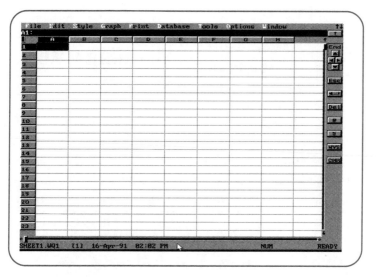

Figure 3-4. *Displaying the date and time on your worksheet screen.*

Selecting Menu Options Using The Mouse

You can move the mouse pointer without moving the cursor to select a menu option. The pointer need only be in the same area as the option when you click for the option to work.

In this lesson you learned how to open a menu and select menu options using the keyboard or the mouse. In the next lesson you will learn how to split a worksheet screen.

Lesson 4
Working with Windows

In this lesson you'll learn how to split a worksheet into two separate panes, synchronize and unsynchronize the panes, and return the worksheet to a single window.

Splitting Large Worksheets

Because worksheets can contain information beyond that which you can see on a single screen, Quattro Pro includes a way to look at more than one portion of the worksheet simultaneously. Figure 4-1 shows a worksheet that contains more entries than can be seen on-screen.

Windows and Panes A window contains a single worksheet in which you can open a pane. A pane enables you to see different parts of a worksheet or several worksheets all in one window.

Suppose that you are working on the Expense portion of a worksheet. As shown in Figure 4.2, when you move down to the expense area, the month names in row 2 disappear. This makes it difficult to tell if you are entering the numbers into the correct month. In cases such as this, Quattro Pro allows you to split the screen at row 2 so that you can see the month names at all times, using the following steps:

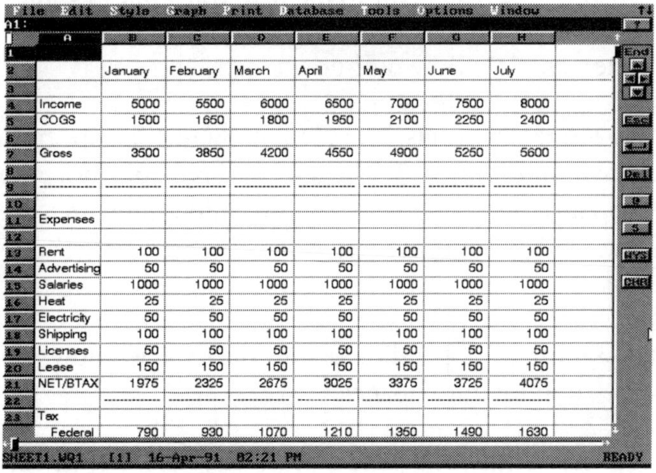

File Edit Style Graph Print Database Tools Options Window

A1:

	A	B	C	D	E	F	G	H
1								
2		January	February	March	April	May	June	July
3								
4	Income	5000	5500	6000	6500	7000	7500	8000
5	COGS	1500	1650	1800	1950	2100	2250	2400
6								
7	Gross	3500	3850	4200	4550	4900	5250	5600
8								
9	------------	------------	------------	------------	------------	------------	------------	------------
10								
11	Expenses							
12								
13	Rent	100	100	100	100	100	100	100
14	Advertising	50	50	50	50	50	50	50
15	Salaries	1000	1000	1000	1000	1000	1000	1000
16	Heat	25	25	25	25	25	25	25
17	Electricity	50	50	50	50	50	50	50
18	Shipping	100	100	100	100	100	100	100
19	Licenses	50	50	50	50	50	50	50
20	Lease	150	150	150	150	150	150	150
21	NET/BTAX	1975	2325	2675	3025	3375	3725	4075
22		------------	------------	------------	------------	------------	------------	------------
23	Tax							
24	Federal	790	930	1070	1210	1350	1490	1630

SHEET1.WQ1 [1] 16-Apr-91 02:21 PM READY

Figure 4-1. *A large worksheet.*

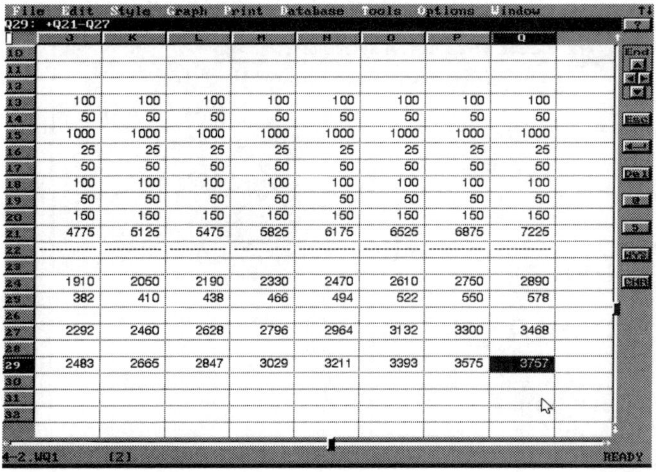

File Edit Style Graph Print Database Tools Options Window

Q29: +Q21-Q27

	J	K	L	M	N	O	P	Q
10								
11								
12								
13	100	100	100	100	100	100	100	100
14	50	50	50	50	50	50	50	50
15	1000	1000	1000	1000	1000	1000	1000	1000
16	25	25	25	25	25	25	25	25
17	50	50	50	50	50	50	50	50
18	100	100	100	100	100	100	100	100
19	50	50	50	50	50	50	50	50
20	150	150	150	150	150	150	150	150
21	4775	5125	5475	5825	6175	6525	6875	7225
22	------------	------------	------------	------------	------------	------------	------------	------------
23								
24	1910	2050	2190	2330	2470	2610	2750	2890
25	382	410	438	466	494	522	550	578
26								
27	2292	2460	2628	2796	2964	3132	3300	3468
28								
29	2483	2665	2847	3029	3211	3393	3575	3757
30								
31								
32								

4-2.WQ1 [2] READY

Figure 4-2. *Moving down the worksheet makes column titles disappear.*

1. Move the cell selector to the row you want to split.

2. Select the Window pull-down menu.

3. Now select Options. The Options submenu appears, as shown in Figure 4-3. The cursor is now positioned on the Horizontal option. The description in the message line reads Split window horizontally at cursor position.

4. Press Enter. You should now have a window split horizontally into 2 panes.

5. To move between panes, press F6. The cell selector jumps to the bottom pane.

6. Press PgDn twice.

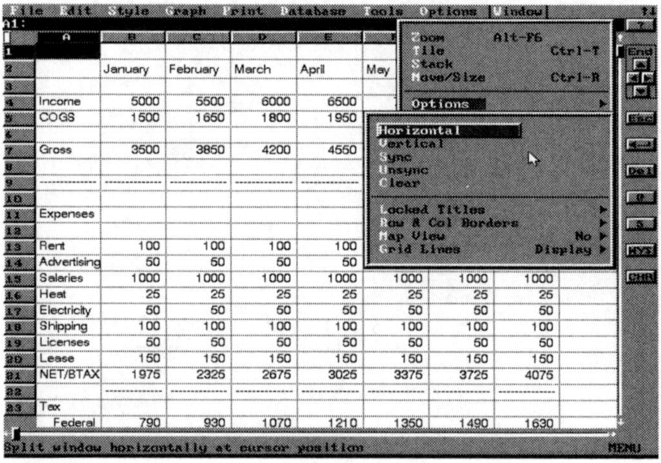

Figure 4-3. The Options submenu.

Notice that the row numbers are no longer in sequence and that you can see the bottom portion of the worksheet.

The month names are still visible. With the screen split into two panes, information can be entered easily.

Unsynchronizing Panes

The default setting for panes is synchronized. That is, if you move the cell selector from left to right, both panes move in concert. Perform the following steps to see how synchronized windows work:

1. Press Tab. Notice that the column letters at the cell selector location are the same.

2. Press Shift+Tab. The cell selector is now back where you started.

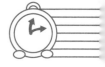

   Shift+Tab Shift+Tab is an example of a *key combination*. When you see two key names together with a + (plus sign) in between, simply press and hold these two keys simultaneously. Do not press the + (plus sign) in between.

   To unsynchronize the two panes, use the following steps:

1. Select the Window pull-down menu.

2. Now select Options.

3. From the Options submenu select the Unsync option.

4. Press Tab twice. Now the column numbers are no longer identical. The top pane shows the top left corner of the worksheet, while the bottom pane displays the bottom right portion of the worksheet. To resynchronize the panes, select the Sync option on the Options submenu.

Removing a Split To remove a split, simply select the Window pull-down menu, select Options, and then Clear from the Options submenu.

Vertically Splitting Worksheets

You can also split a worksheet vertically so that you can see a second set of row numbers within a worksheet. To do this, follow these steps:

1. Position the cell selector in the column you want to split.

2. Select the Window pull-down menu.

3. Now select Options.

4. Select the Vertical option from the Options submenu. The screen is now split vertically as in Figure 4-4.

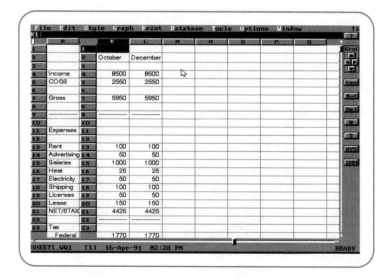

Figure 4-4. A vertically split screen.

Removing Row and Column Borders

To get a better idea of what your printed worksheet will look like, follow these steps to remove the row and column borders:

1. Select the Window pull-down menu.

2. Now select Options.

3. Select the Row & Column Borders option from the Options submenu and press Enter.

4. Now select the Hide option. The screen should now resemble Figure 4-5.

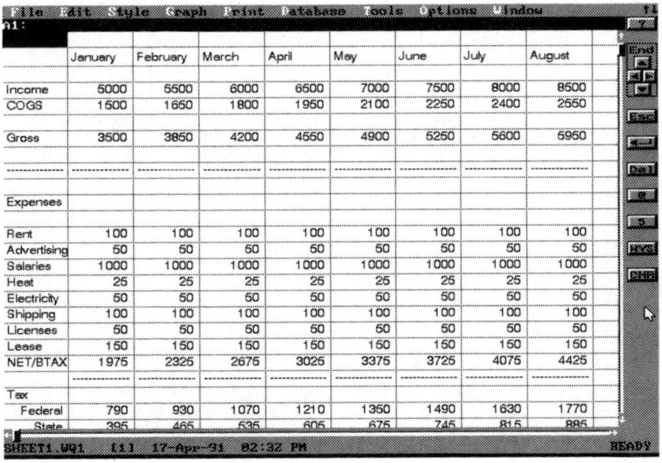

Figure 4-5. A worksheet with the Row & Column Borders removed.

Another way to see what your worksheet will look like when printed is to use the Print Preview option, discussed in Lesson 15.

In this lesson you learned how to split a single worksheet horizontally and vertically, and remove the row and column borders from the worksheet screen. In the next lesson you will learn how to enter labels and values into your worksheets.

Lesson 5
Entering Labels and Values

In this lesson you'll learn how to enter labels (text) and values (numbers) into worksheet cells.

Entering a Label

To enter a label simply move the cell selector to the cell location and type the information. To enter a label in cell B1, for example, follow these steps:

1. Move the cell selector to cell B1.

2. Type the label text. (For this example, type **LABELS AND DATA**.) Notice that the letters appear on the Input line, and not in the worksheet. Quattro Pro allows you to see what the entry will look like before putting it into the worksheet, to give you an opportunity to edit.

3. Press Enter. The worksheet should resemble Figure 5-1.

As you typed your label, a *cursor* appeared on the Input line. After you type a character, the cursor automatically moves to the next character position.

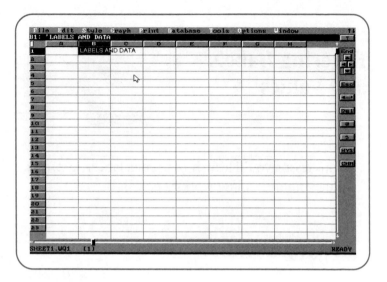

Figure 5-1. *The title LABELS AND DATA entered into cell B1.*

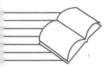

The Input Line Cursor The Input Line cursor is the blinking dash positioned at the bottom of the rectangular highlight.

When you enter a label into a cell, Quattro Pro automatically left aligns that label in the cell. If you enter one of the following formatting characters before the label itself, you can control the label's alignment:

'   Left-aligned text (default)

^   Centered text

"   Right-aligned text

Entering Values as Labels

By default, Quattro Pro interprets any value that begins with a number as a value. You can use the label prefixes to trick Quattro Pro into displaying a value as a label. For instance, if you wanted to enter 16 March as a label, you would use the following steps:

1. Move the cell selector to the cell you want to make the entry in.

2. Type `'16 March`.

3. Press Enter, or a direction key. The leading apostrophe tricks Quattro Pro into displaying the entry as a label.

Insert and OverStrike

There are two keyboard modes for entering information: insert and overstrike. The default mode is insert so that when you type a character, it is inserted at the cursor position. Any characters to the right of the cursor are pushed forward. In overstrike mode, characters typed appear at the cursor position and overwrite existing characters. To change the default entry mode, press Insert.

Long Cell Entries

In Figure 5-1, it looks like the entry in cell B1 has spilled over into cell C1. To check and see, move the cell selector to cell C1. Notice that there is no entry in cell C1, according to the Input line at the top of the screen. Quattro Pro allows long label entries to appear in adjoining cells as long as there is no entry in the adjoining cell. To see the effect of

35

making an entry where a long label appears, type`This is a test` into cell C2. Press ←. Your screen should resemble Figure 5-2.

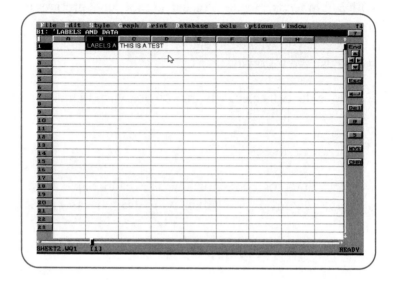

Figure 5-2. The label can't spill over into cell C2.

In the Input line, the full label is displayed. But, in cell B2 you can only see a portion, while the words `This is a test` appear in cell C2.

Entering Values

Quattro Pro checks to see if you are entering a label, number, or formula. In the first example, Quattro Pro automatically recognized that you were entering a label because the first key pressed was a letter, or a label prefix. Enter values the same way, as follows:

1. Move the cell selector to the cell you want to place the value in.

2. Type the value.

3. Press Enter or a direction key. The value appears in the cell as in Figure 5-3.

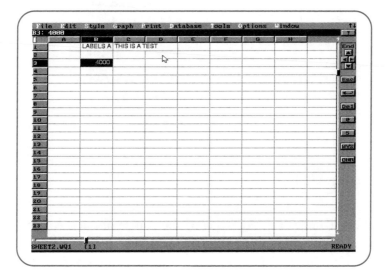

Figure 5-3. A value (number) entered into a cell.

Notice the Input line and the cell display. Refer to Lesson 9 to find out how to enter values as part of formulas.

In this lesson you learned how to enter labels and values into cells and differentiate between alignment styles offered. In the next lesson you will learn how to save and close a worksheet.

Lesson 6
Saving and Closing a Worksheet

In this lesson you'll learn how to save and close a worksheet to remove it from the screen.

Saving a Worksheet for the First Time

When Quattro Pro saves a worksheet, it creates a file of the worksheet and stores the file on a disk you specify. Periodically saving a worksheet, even when you are not finished working with it, is a good idea. If you don't save frequently, power failures and accidental machine shutdowns can cause you to lose your work.

For Safety's Sake You should save your worksheet files every 5-10 minutes.

When you save a worksheet, you must specify a name for the worksheet file. Type in a file name of up to eight characters. Quattro Pro automatically adds a .WQ1 extension to the the file name. You can use the following characters in file names:

Letters A through Z (uppercase or lowercase)

Numbers 0 through 9

These symbols: ! @ # $ % ^ & ( ) - _

The following characters are not allowed: space ~ + =
| \ / ? <>, . { }

If you try to use an incorrect character, Quattro Pro beeps and displays the message `Invalid character in file name`. If this message appears, press Esc and start over.

To save a worksheet file, follow these steps:

1. Select the File pull-down menu.

2. Select the Save option. The Save File dialog box appears as in Figure 6-1. The first line reads `Enter save file name`. Underneath is the path in which Quattro Pro is installed, and the default file search.

3. If you are satisfied with the path that Quattro Pro has chosen, you need only type in the name of the file. If you wish to change the path, press Esc 3 times. The suggested path is erased and you can begin entering a new path. Press Enter to accept the file name and save the file to disk.

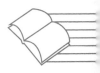

Path.. The path is what you tell Quattro Pro to follow to save or retrieve a file. This path includes the drive (usually A:, B:, or C;) and directory (and subdirectories).

Brushing Up on Directory Basics If the whole idea of working with drives and directories is confusing, use the DOS Primer in the back of this book.

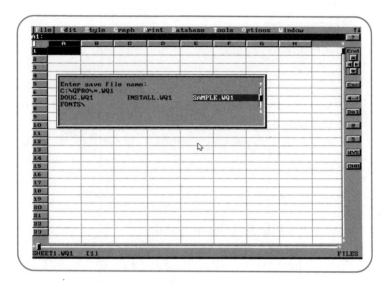

Figure 6-1. *The Save File dialog box.*

Saving a Worksheet That Already Exists

As you make changes to a worksheet, you need to save them. It only takes a moment once the worksheet has been named. You can use the following shortcut key combination:

1. Press Ctrl+S. Because the worksheet has been saved before, Quattro Pro displays the File Already Exists dialog box shown in Figure 6-2.

   The options in this dialog box are as follows:

   Cancel   Returns you to the worksheet

   Replace   Overwrites the previously saved version of the worksheet

Backup   Saves the current version of the worksheet with the .WQ1 extension, and modifies the file extension on the 1st version from .WQ1 to .BAK

2. Select the appropriate option.

3. Press Enter to complete the save.

Using Save As You can select Save as from the File pull-down menu to save the current (revised) version with a .WQ1 extension and the old version with a .BAK extension.

Figure 6-2. The File Already Exists dialog box.

Closing a Worksheet File

Closing a worksheet file removes it from the screen. Be sure to save your work before you use the following steps for closing a worksheet:

41

1. Select the File pull-down menu.

2. Select the Close option. If you have made changes to the worksheet, Quattro Pro prompts you with a dialog box asking, Lose your changes? Selecting Yes closes the worksheet and does not save any changes. Selecting No closes the menu and takes you back into the worksheet.

If you have several open worksheets, you can close them all at once (save your work first). To close multiple worksheets, follow these steps:

1. Select the File pull-down menu.

2. Select the Close All option.

If changes have been made to the worksheet, Quattro Pro prompts you to save it.

In this lesson you learned how to save and close a worksheet. In the next lesson you will learn how to open a new or existing worksheet.

Lesson 7
Opening and Using Worksheets

In this lesson you'll learn how to open a new worksheet, and retrieve an existing worksheet.

Opening a New Worksheet

When you start Quattro Pro, it automatically opens a worksheet called SHEET1.WQ1. The name of the worksheet is displayed in the lower left corner of the worksheet screen as in Figure 7-1.

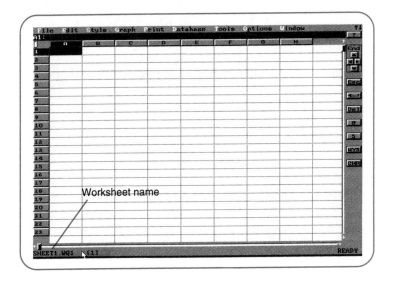

Worksheet name

Figure 7-1. The SHEET.WQ1 worksheet.

43

The name, SHEET1.WQ1, is generic. Quattro Pro assumes you will add a specific name to every worksheet you create.

Quattro Pro allows you to have up to 32 worksheets open at once. This means that you can have many different types of worksheets instantly available on your screen. Each worksheet occupies a separate window.

Look at Figure 7-1. Notice that just after the name SHEET.WQ1 is the number 1, enclosed in brackets [1]. This is Quattro Pro's way of letting you know which window is active. As you open more worksheets, the number in the bracket increases. Now open a new worksheet, which means that a second worksheet window is also being opened. Use the following steps:

1. Select the File pull-down menu.

2. The cursor is on the New option. The description line in the lower left corner of the screen reads Open a new blank spreadsheet window.

3. Press Enter. Your screen should now look like Figure 7-2.

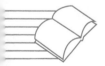

What's Its Name? The terms spreadsheet and worksheet are synonymous.

Look at the bottom left corner of the screen. It now reads SHEET2.WQ1 [2]. The [2] indicates that you are now working in a second worksheet window.

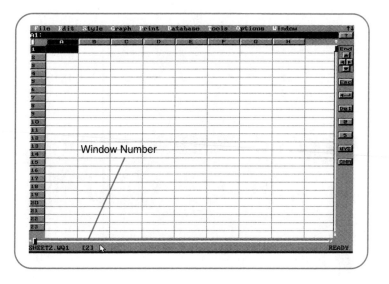

Figure 7-2. Opening a new worksheet.

Tiling and Changing Windows

Use the Window pull-down menu to manipulate the windows that are open. You can zoom, tile, stack, or resize windows. However, when the screen is displayed in WYSIWYG mode, you cannot stack windows. Use the following steps to tile a window:

1. Select the Window pull-down menu. The Window pull-down menu appears, as shown in Figure 7-3.

2. Select the Tile option. Your screen should look like Figure 7-4.

    Switching Windows To switch between windows use Shift+F6.

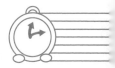

45

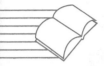

Tiling Windows When you are working with multiple worksheets, the Tile option arranges the worksheet windows so that a portion of each worksheet is on-screen. Use Ctrl+T to access the Tile option quickly.

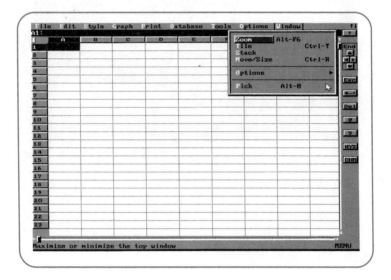

Figure 7-3. *The Window pull-down menu.*

As you can see by the titles in the upper left corner of each worksheet window, SHEET2.WQ1 appears on the left side of the screen. SHEET1.WQ1 is on the right. Quattro Pro indicates that SHEET2.WQ1 is the active worksheet window by displaying the name in the lower left corner of the screen. Because SHEET2.WQ1 is the active worksheet window, you could begin typing information into it. To activate another worksheet window (in this case, SHEET1.WQ1), use the following steps:

1. Select the Window pull-down menu.

2. Select the Pick option. Quattro Pro displays the Pick dialog box listing the two open worksheets.

46

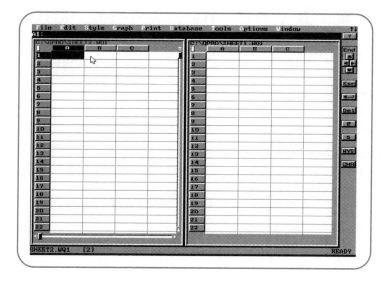

Figure 7-4. Tiled worksheets.

3. Select the worksheet you want to activate (SHEET1.WQ1 for example).

The cursor jumps to cell A1 in SHEET1.WQ1, and the name SHEET1.WQ1 is displayed in the lower left corner of the screen.

Zooming a Window

Now suppose that you want to return a tiled worksheet window (like SHEET1.WQ1) to full screen size. This process is called *zooming* a window. You can use the Window pull-down menu to effect the zoom, or use a speed key combination as follows:

1. Activate the worksheet window you want to zoom (SHEET1.WQ1).

2. Now press Alt+F6. The active worksheet window (SHEET1.WQ1) expands to full-screen size.

Stacking Windows

If you are operating Quattro Pro in character mode, you can stack the worksheet windows so that the worksheets look like stacked file folders. Use the following steps:

1. Select the Window pull-down menu.

2. Select the Stack option. The worksheet windows stack, as shown in Figure 7-5.

I Can't Stack! Remember, if you are currently in WYSIWYG mode, you cannot stack windows!

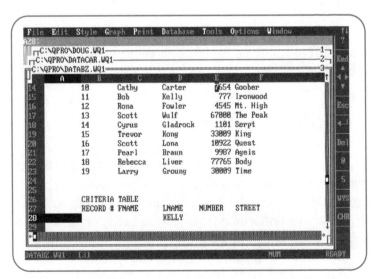

Figure 7-5. The stacked worksheet windows.

48

Opening an Existing Worksheet

When you open an existing worksheet you've previously saved, Quattro Pro also places it in its own new window. To open an existing worksheet, use the following steps:

1. Select the File pull-down menu.

   Quattro Pro offers two options for bringing a saved file to the worksheet window:

   • The Open option, which loads the saved file into a new worksheet window.

   • The Retrieve option, which loads the saved file into the active worksheet window.

   If you select the Retrieve option, any information already in the active worksheet window is replaced by the saved file. Unless you are certain that the information in the active worksheet window is not needed, use the Open option.

2. Select the Open option. Quattro Pro displays the File Open dialog box, which includes a list of subdirectories and files, as in Figure 7-6.

3. Switch directories, if necessary, by selecting another directory and pressing Enter.

4. Select a file name and press Enter. Quattro Pro retrieves the stored file from disk and displays the worksheet on-screen. Notice that the file name is displayed in the lower left corner of the screen along with the window number.

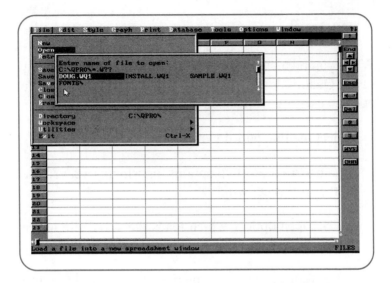

Figure 7-6. *The File Open dialog box.*

In this lesson you learned how to open a new worksheet, retrieve a saved worksheet, and tile, zoom, and stack multiple worksheets. In the next lesson you will learn how to work with cell blocks.

Lesson 8
Selecting, Moving, Copying, and Naming Cell Blocks

In this lesson you'll learn how to select a block of cells and then move or copy the information to a different part of the worksheet.

Selecting Cell Blocks

A block of cells is one or more adjacent cells. The cells selected must be in a rectangular pattern. To select a group of cells, simply highlight the cells you want to work with. A block can consist of a single cell or the entire worksheet. Selecting cells can be accomplished using the following steps:

1. Move the cell pointer to the cell that you want to use as the first cell in the block.

2. Press Shift+F7. EXT appears in the Mode Indicator letting you know that Quattro Pro is in Extend mode.

3. Use the direction keys to expand the highlight over the cells you want to select. The cells must be adjacent and in a square or rectangular shape.

With the cell block selected, you can move, copy, delete, transpose, fill the block with a series of values, search, replace, or create a block name. To exit the EXT mode, press Esc.

Pointing a Block

If you have accessed the Edit pull-down menu and selected one of the block options before selecting a block, Quattro Pro prompts you for a block of cells on which to execute the option. You can type the cell address, A1..B16, or expand the cell block by highlighting the cells with the cell pointer.

If the cell pointer is not in the correct cell when you begin the operation, press Esc to unanchor the cell pointer and then move to the beginning cell in the block. Press . (period) to reanchor the cell pointer and select the cell block.

Selecting a Block with the Mouse

Selecting blocks using a mouse is faster than using the direction keys. To select a block with the mouse, use the following steps:

1. Move the mouse pointer to the cell in the upper left corner of the block you want to select.

2. Press and hold the left mouse button (or whichever button is the active button). Quattro Pro is in Extend mode.

3. Drag the mouse pointer to the bottom right cell in the cell block.

4. Release the mouse button.

Selecting a Block with the Mouse Palette

The Mouse Palette includes a set of direction buttons at the top pointing left, right, up and, down. Clicking on one of the direction buttons moves the cell pointer to the first cell containing information in that direction. If no cells contain information, the cell pointer moves to the worksheet border.

Quickly Selecting a Cell Block Use End and a direction button in the Mouse Palette to quickly select a cell block. For example, if the mouse pointer is in the top left cell of the block and you want to extend the highlight down to cover all cells with entries, press End+ a direction button. Quattro Pro automatically highlights all cells below the current cell until it finds a blank cell.

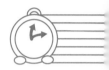

Moving a Cell Block

If you want to change the location of a block of cells, simply use Quattro Pro's Move option to relocate the whole block of cells at once. When you move (or copy) a cell block, it overwrites any information in the destination cells. If you accidentally overwrite data when moving or copying cells, you can use Quattro Pro's undo feature to revoke the operation.

Use the following steps to move a cell block:

1. Move the cell selector to the cell block which contains the information you want to move. The Input line at the top of the screen displays the cell's contents.

2. Select the Edit pull-down menu. The Edit pull-down menu is displayed in Figure 8-1.

3. Select the Move option. The Input line message reads `Source block of cells:` followed by the current location of the cell selector. The *source block* contains the cells you want to move.

4. Press the direction keys or drag the highlight with the mouse to extend the cell block. In Figure 8-2, both cells A1 and A2 are highlighted.

5. Press Enter. The message in the Input line now reads `Destination for cells: A1`.

6. Move the cell selector to the upper left cell of the *destination block* (cell E1 in our example worksheet).

7. Press Enter. Quattro Pro moves the source block data to the destination block. Figure 8.3 shows the result of moving cell block A1..A2 to cell block E1..E2.

Undoing Your Mistakes Turn on Quattro Pro's undo feature by selecting the Options pull-down menu, the Other option, the Undo option and then the Enable command. You can then use Alt+F5 to undo Quatto Pro operations. To make sure undo will remain enabled for future work sessions, choose the Options pull-down menu and then the Update option.

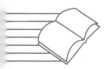

Source and Destination Blocks The source block contains the cell or cells that you want to move. The destination block is where you want the cell or cells to be moved to.

Shortcut Press Ctrl+M to access the Move option quickly.

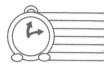

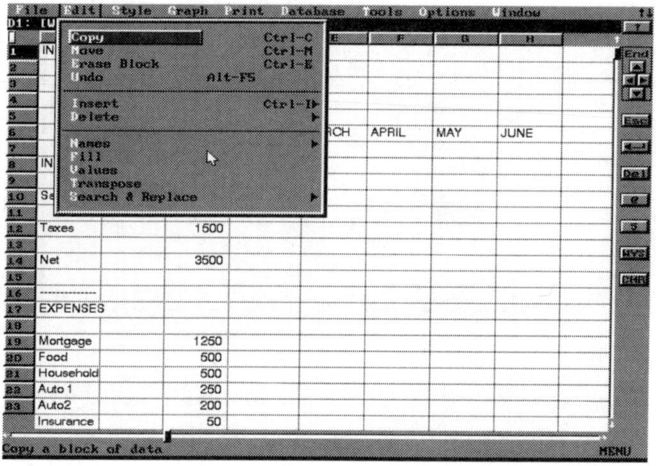

File	Edit	Style	Graph	Print	Database	Tools	Options	Window	
D1: [U									

	Copy		Ctrl-C	E	F	G	H
1	IN	**Move**		Ctrl-M			
2		**Erase Block**		Ctrl-E			
3		**Undo**		Alt-F5			
4							
5		**Insert**		Ctrl-I▶			
6		**Delete**		▶	RCH	APRIL	MAY	JUNE
7							
8	IN	**Names**		▶			
9		**Fill**					
10	Sa	**Values**					
11		**Transpose**					
11		**Search & Replace**		▶			
12	Taxes		1500				
13							
14	Net		3500				
15							
16	---------						
17	EXPENSES						
18							
19	Mortgage		1250				
20	Food		500				
21	Household		500				
22	Auto 1		250				
23	Auto2		200				
	Insurance		50				

Copy a block of data   MENU

Figure 8-1. The Edit pull-down menu.

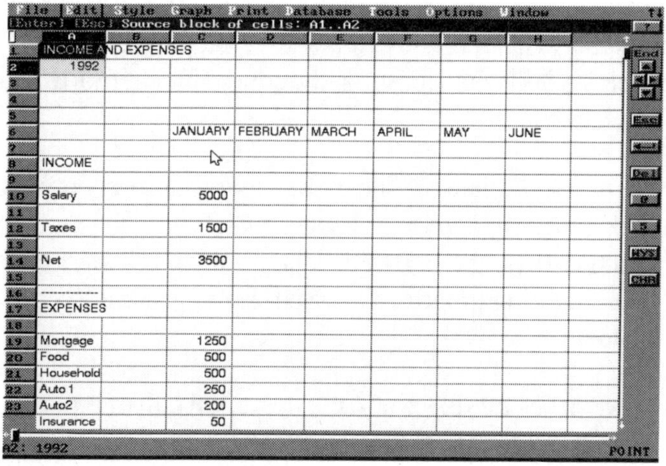

File	Edit	Style	Graph	Print	Database	Tools	Options	Window	
[Enter] [Esc] Source block of cells: A1..A2									

	A	B	C	D	E	F	G	H
1	INCOME AND EXPENSES							
2	1992							
3								
4								
5								
6			JANUARY	FEBRUARY	MARCH	APRIL	MAY	JUNE
7								
8	INCOME							
9								
10	Salary		5000					
11								
12	Taxes		1500					
13								
14	Net		3500					
15								
16	---------							
17	EXPENSES							
18								
19	Mortgage		1250					
20	Food		500					
21	Household		500					
22	Auto 1		250					
23	Auto2		200					
	Insurance		50					

A2: 1992   POINT

Figure 8-2. Cells A1 and A2 highlighted.

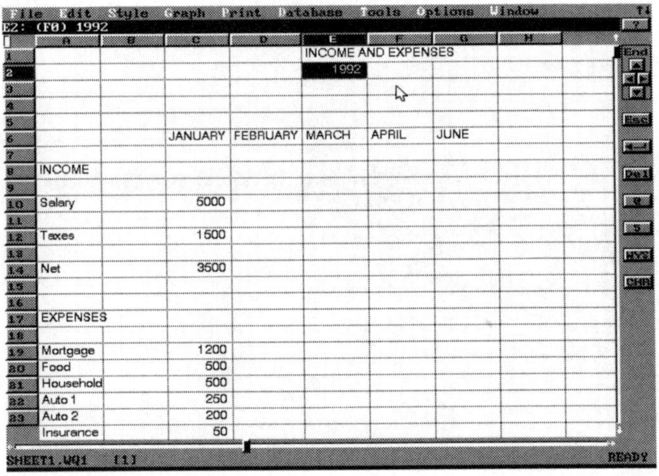

Figure 8-3. Cell block A1..A2 moved to cell block E1..E2.

Copying Cells

The distinction between copying and moving cell information is that when copying, the source block information is not deleted and when moving, the source block information is deleted.

In the example worksheet, the income and expenses are entered for a single month. Rather than typing the contents across the rows, the copy command makes it a snap to fill in the remaining months. Use the following steps to copy a cell block:

1. Move the cell selector to the upper left cell of the source block.

2. Select the Edit pull-down menu.

3. Select the Copy option. Quattro Pro prompts you for the source block cells. In Figure 8-4, a large block has been selected as the copy source block.

4. Press the direction keys or drag the mouse pointer until the cell selector highlights all the cells you want to copy.

5. Press Enter. Quattro Pro prompts you for the copy destination block.

6. Move the cell selector to the copy destination.

7. Press the . (period) to anchor the cell selector.

8. Move the cell selector to highlight the destination block. Figure 8-5 shows a large block of cells highlighted to receive the copy.

9. Press Enter. Quattro Pro copies the cells from the source block to the cells in the destination block.

Shortcut Pressing Ctrl+C accesses the Copy option quickly.

Creating Block Names

An alternative to entering cell addresses is to create a name for a block of cells. After creating block names, you can use them in formulas as if they were the cell addresses. For example, if you had a block of cells named EXPENSES and one named TOTALS, you could enter a formula such as: +TOTALS–EXPENSES and the values in the cells would be used to make the calculations.

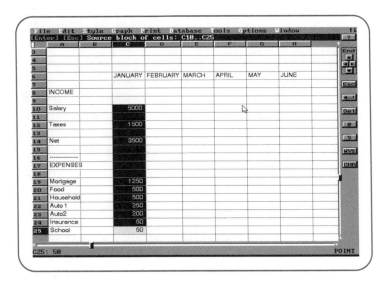

Figure 8-4. *A column selected for copying.*

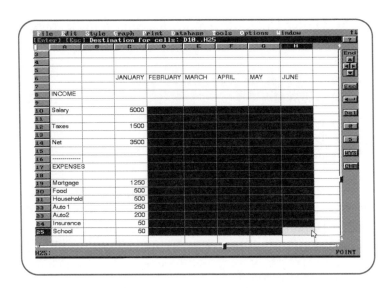

Figure 8-5. *The cell block D10..H25 highlighted.*

To create a block name, use the following steps:

1. Select the Edit pull-down menu.

2. Select the Names option.

3. From the Names submenu, select the Create option. A dialog box appears asking you to enter a name of up to 15 characters in length.

4. Press Enter. Quattro Pro returns you to the worksheet and prompts you to enter a block of cells. After entering the cell block, press Enter.

Making A Table of Block Names

After you have created several named blocks, you can print a list of block names and their addresses so you can easily reference the block names. To do this, use the following steps:

1. Select the Edit pull-down menu.

2. Select the Names option.

3. From the Names submenu, select the Create Table option.

4. Quattro Pro returns you to the worksheet. The table consists of two columns: the first contains the names, the second the cell block addresses. Position the cell pointer in a portion of the worksheet where it will not overwrite any existing data, and press Enter.

In this lesson you learned how to select a block of cells for either moving or copying. In the next lesson you will learn how to enter formulas and functions.

Lesson 9
Entering Formulas and Functions

In this lesson you'll learn how to enter formulas, combine them with Quattro Pro's built-in financial functions and adjust the recalculation options.

Entering Formulas

The heart of a worksheet is its formulas. The key concept in understanding how to enter a formula is that, instead of entering the actual numbers themselves, you enter the cell addresses, which contain the numbers you want to calculate. Every formula you enter must begin with a plus (+) sign so that Quattro Pro knows it is a formula. Table 9-1 lists the mathematical operators you can use to build Quattro Pro formulas and their precedence.

Table 9-1. Mathematical Operators.

Operator	Description	Precedence
&	Links two labels	1
#AND#, #OR#	Logical AND, Logical OR	1
#NOT#	Logical NOT	2
=, < >	Equal, Not equal	3
<, >	Less than, Greater than	3

Operator	Description	Precedence
<=	Less than or Equal to	3
>=	Greater than or Equal to	3
−, +	Subtraction, Addition	4
*, /	Multiplication, Division	5
−, +	Negative, Positive	6
^	Exponentiation	7

Operators that have the identical level of precedence are calculated in order from left to right. To change the order of calculation, enclose the formula you want calculated first in parentheses.

Use the following steps to create a formula:

1. Move the cell selector to the cell where you want the result of the formula to be displayed.

2. Type + (plus sign). This alerts Quattro Pro that a formula is to follow.

3. After the + (plus sign), type the cell addresses that you want to sum. For example, if you want to total the values in cells A1 and B1, and want the result in cell C1, with the cell selector in cell C1, you would type+A1+B1 .

4. Press Enter. Quattro Pro displays the formula result in the cell where you entered the formula. For example, the result is displayed in cell C1, and the formula is displayed in the Input line, as shown in Figure 9-1.

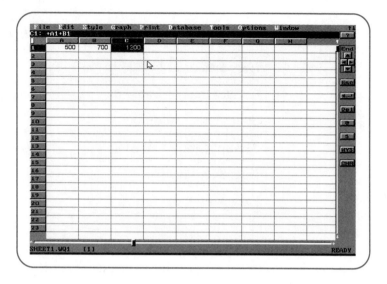

Figure 9-1. The formula result shown in cell C1 and the formula in the Input line.

If you are only totaling two cells, it is easy to type in the cell addresses by hand. But for many cells, this is unrealistic. The @SUM function can total a block of cells. The following steps explain how to enter a function using the @SUM function:

1. Move the cell selector to the cell where you want the total to display.

2. Type @SUM(.

3. Move the cell selector to the cell containing the first value you want to total. In Figure 9-2, the function formula is entered and the cell selector is positioned on the first value to be included in the block.

4. Press . (period) to anchor the cell selector.

5. Use the direction keys or drag the mouse pointer to expand the highlight so that it includes all of the cells you want to total.

6. Type).

7. Press Enter. The total appears in the cell where the formula is located and the Input line displays the complete function formula.

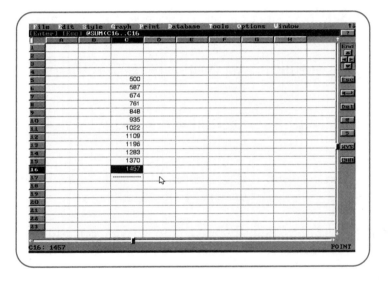

Figure 9-2. *A column of values with the @SUM function formula entered.*

Use Quattro Pro's built-in functions and your own formulas to create powerful financial models.

Recalculation Options

Quattro Pro recalculates the formulas in a worksheet every time you make a new cell entry or cell edit (see Lesson 11

63

for information on editing cells). However, on a large worksheet, you may not want Quattro Pro to recalculate until you have made all of your edits. To modify the recalculation options, use the following steps:

1. Select the Options pull-down menu.

2. Select the Recalculation option. The Recalculation submenu appears, as shown in Figure 9-3.

3. Select the Mode option. Three options are presented in the submenu:

Automatic   Automatically recalculates all affected formulas

Manual   Recalculates affected formulas when you press F9

Background   Recalculates all affected formulas between keystrokes

4. Select the Manual option. Now Quattro Pro will only recalculate the worksheet when you press F9.

In this lesson you learned how to enter simple formulas and functions, and use the Recalculation option. In the next lesson you will learn how to build more sophisticated worksheets with absolute cell references.

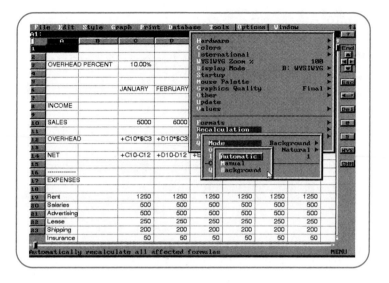

Figure 9-3. The Recalculation submenu.

Lesson 10
Using Absolute Cell References

In this lesson you'll learn how to differentiate between absolute and relative references.

Absolute or Relative?

When you copy formulas, Quattro Pro adjusts the cell references in the formulas relative to their new positions in the worksheet. In most instances, this is what you want to have happen. For example, in Figure 10-1, the cell formulas containing the totals for February through June (columns D-H) were copied from the formula in the January column total. If the formulas did not adjust, the totals would be identical in every month.

Suppose that you want to copy a formula that refers to the same cell in every case. An example of such a situation is where the formula calculates a specific percentage of the cell's value. Formulas in multiple cells could refer to a percentage stored in one cell. In Figure 10-2, the percentage of overhead charged to each month's expenses is calculated by multiplying the number in the SALES row by the percentage stored in cell C3.

As they appear in Figure 10-2, the formulas in cells D12 through H12 are incorrect. Those formulas copied from cell C12 do not reference the correct cell (C3) containing the overhead percentage.

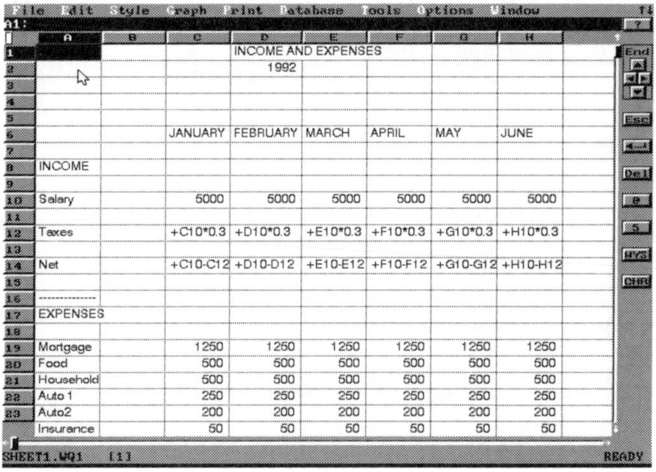

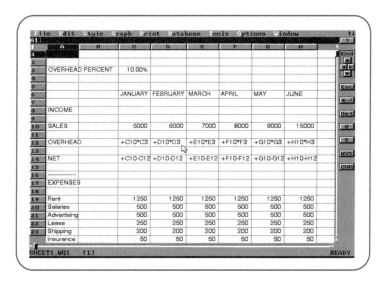

Figure 10-1. *Relative formulas across the months.*

Figure 10-2. *The copied formulas incorrectly adjusted.*

To make a cell reference absolute, you add a $ (dollar sign) to the cell address. You can enter the $ (dollar sign) when you type the formula, or retroactively insert it if you discover an incorrect calculation result. Follow these steps to make a reference absolute:

1. Move the cell selector to the cell containing the formula references you want to make absolute.

2. Press F2 to put Quattro Pro into Edit mode.

3. Move the cursor to the cell address you want to make absolute.

4. Press F4, the Absolute Value key. Pressing it once makes both the column letter and row number of the cell reference absolute. Pressing it again makes only the row reference absolute. Pressing F4 once more makes the column reference absolute.

In Figure 10-2, cell C12's column reference to the second cell address (C3) must be made absolute so that when the formula is copied across the row, the formula correctly refers to the percentage value in cell C3. Figure 10-3 displays the copied formulas with the column references absolute.

In this lesson you learned how to add absolute references to a formula. In the next lesson you will learn how to edit cell entries.

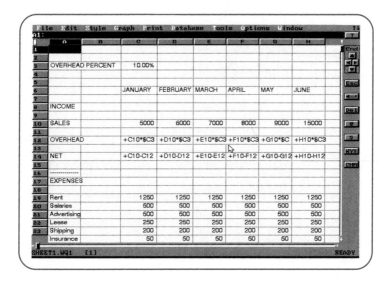

Figure 10-3. *Column reference formulas made absolute.*

In this lesson you'll learn how to edit a cell entry and delete cell contents.

Editing a Cell

After you have made an entry to a cell and inserted it into the worksheet, you may discover it needs to be corrected. Table 11-1 defines the use of keys in Edit mode:

Table 11-1. The Edit Mode Keys.

Push	To
←	Move cursor left one character
→	Move cursor right one character
Home	Move cursor to the beginning of the Input line
End	Move cursor to the end of the entry
Tab	Move cursor right 5 characters
Shift+Tab	Move cursor left 5 characters
Del	Delete character at the cursor position
Backspace	Delete character to the left of the cursor position
Escape	Erase the entire entry
Enter	Accept an edit

To edit an entry, use the following steps:

1. Move the cell selector to the cell containing the entry to be edited.

2. Press F2. Quattro Pro is now in Edit mode. Instead of a cell selector in the worksheet, Quattro Pro displays a cursor in the Input line at the end of the cell entry, as shown in Figure 11-1. The Edit indicator appears in the lower right corner of the screen, as shown in Figure 11-2.

3. Edit the cell contents shown in the Input line using the keys listed in Table 11-1, if necessary.

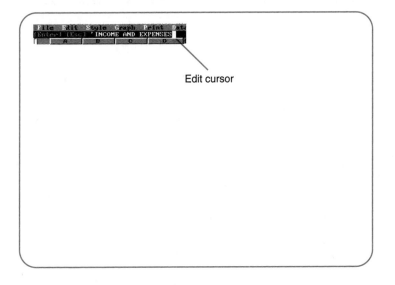

Edit cursor

Figure 11-1. Editing an entry on the Input line.

Deleting Cell Contents Move the cell selector to the cell that contains the information you want to delete. Press Del.

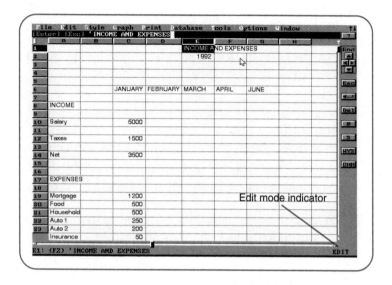

Figure 11-2. The Edit Mode Indicator.

Deleting the Contents of a Cell Block

When you need to delete the contents of many cells, follow these steps:

1. Move the cell selector to the first cell that you want to modify.

2. Select the Edit pull-down menu.

3. Select the Erase Block option.

4. Use the direction keys or drag the mouse pointer to expand the highlight to the cells you want to modify.

5. Press Enter.

Lesson 12
Working with Columns and Rows

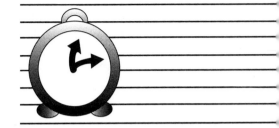

In this lesson you'll learn how to widen specific columns, insert a row or column, delete a row or column and if you are using the WYSIWYG mode of Quattro Pro, change the row height.

Changing Column Width

When you enter a value, or the worksheet calculates one that is too large for Quattro Pro to display in the cell, a series of ****** (asterisks) appear in place of the value. Figure 12.1 shows a worksheet with several values in one column that are too wide for the current column width. To see the values you must increase the column width until it can display the full value. To do this, follow these steps:

1. Move the cell selector to the column that you want to widen.

2. Select the Style pull-down menu. Figure 12-2 shows Quattro Pro's Style pull-down menu.

3. Select the Column Width option. The Input line displays the message `Alter the width of the current column [1..254]` followed by a value that indicates the current width.

4. Type a new value, or use → to widen the column one character at a time.

5. Press Enter. Quattro Pro adjusts the column width and displays values instead of asterisks in cells.

Shortcut Pressing Ctrl+W accesses the Column Width option quickly.

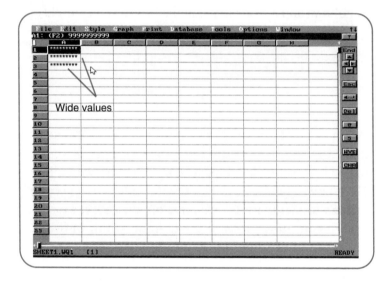

Figure 12-1. A worksheet with several values in one column that are too wide for the current column width.

Inserting a Row or Column

When you need to insert a row or column, Quattro Pro allows you to do so without damaging any cell references you have previously entered. If you insert a row or column within a block that is used in a formula, Quattro Pro adjusts the formula to include the new column or row. For example, if the block address is C1..C10 and you insert a new row at row 5, the new block address is C1..C11. The same is true for inserting a column. If the block address is C1..G1 and you insert a new column at column D, the new block address is C1..H1.

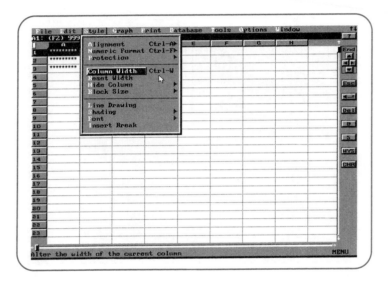

Figure 12-2. *The Style pull-down menu.*

To insert a row or column, use the following steps:

1. Move the cell selector to the row or column where you want to make an insertion.

2. Select the Edit pull-down menu.

3. Select the Insert option. The Insert Rows or Columns submenu, shown in Figure 12-3, appears.

4. From the Insert Rows or Columns submenu, select Rows or Columns.

75

5. To insert a single row or column, press Enter. To insert multiple rows or columns, use ↑, ↓, ← and → to extend the highlight, and then press Enter.

Shortcut Pressing Ctrl+I accesses the Insert Rows or Columns submenu quickly.

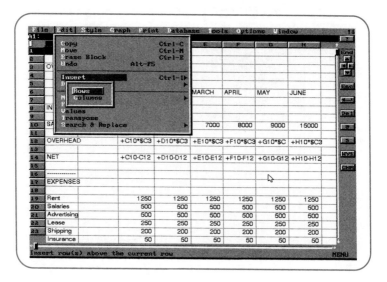

Figure 12-3. The Insert Rows or Columns submenu.

Canceling an Insertion To cancel a row or column insertion, press Esc until you are returned to the Edit pull-down menu.

Deleting Rows or Columns

When you delete a row or column, Quattro Pro adjusts block formulas accordingly. However, be careful when using the Delete option so that you do not cut off a block used as part of a formula calculation.

To delete a row or column:

1. Move the cell selector to the row or column you want to delete.

2. Select the Edit pull-down menu.

3. Select the Delete option.

4. From the Delete submenu, select the Rows or Columns option.

5. To delete a single row or column, press Enter twice. To delete several rows or columns, use the direction keys to extend the highlight and press Enter.

Changing Row Height

In WYSIWYG mode, you can modify the height of a row of cells. To modify the height, use the following the steps:

1. Select the Style pull-down menu.

2. Select the Block Size option.

3. From the Block Size submenu, select the Height option.

4. Select the Set Row Height option.

5. To modify a single row, press Enter and type a *point size* from 1 to 240. To modify several rows, use ↑ and ↓ to extend the highlight over the rows you want to modify. Enter the point size from 1 to 240, and press Enter.

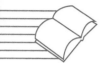

Point Size The size of type (text) is usually measured in points. A point is $^1/_{72}$ of an inch.

The row height setting is saved for a particular worksheet, not as the default. Figure 12-4 shows a worksheet with the height of row A increased to 18 points.

	A	B	C	D	E	F	G	H	
					INCOME AND EXPENSES				
					1992				
			JANUARY	FEBRUARY	MARCH	APRIL	JUNE		
	INCOME								
	Salary		5000						
	Taxes		1500						
	Net		3500						
	EXPENSES								
	Mortgage		1200						
	Food		500						
	Household		500						
	Auto 1		250						
	Auto 2		200						

Figure 12-4. A worksheet with the height of row A increased to 18 points.

In this lesson you learned how to insert or delete a row or column, adjust the width of a column and adjust the height of a row. In the next lesson you will learn how to format labels and values.

Lesson 13

Enhancing the Label and Value Appearance

In this lesson you'll learn how to change fonts, set cell formats, and protect cells.

Setting Value Formats

Value formats can be used to differentiate between types of material, emphasize certain rows or columns or simply improve appearance. Quattro Pro can display values in many recognizable forms, as shown in Table 13-1.

Table 13-1. Value Formats.

Format	Description	Example
Fixed	Displays numbers with a fixed number of decimal places, 0-15.	–234.00 234.67 456789.98
Scientific	Displays numbers in exponential format, including decimal places from 0-15.	–1.7E+9 666E+02 6.66E+09
Currency	Displays numbers in currency format, including the currency symbol and decimal places from 0-15.	($666.00) $999.90 $99,999,999.00

continued

Table 13-1. Continued

Format	Description	Example
, (comma)	Displays numbers including commas to separate thousands, negative values display in parentheses.	(999) 99,999.00
General	Displays numbers with no format.	–456 567.9998 567543.9
+/–	Converts numbers to horizontal bar graphs; either plus signs (+) for positive values, or minus signs (–) for negative values.	++++ ––––
Percent	Displays numbers as a percentage, including decimal places from 0-15.	34.89% 9.96% 11.00%

Date — Displays dates in one of the following formats:

1-(DD-MMM-YY)	Day-Month-Year	16-03-56
2-(DD-MMM)	Day-Month	16-03
3-(MMM-YY)	Month-Year	03-56
4-(Long intl.)	Long international format	12/28/55 87-12-30
5-(Short intl.)	Short international format	12/30 2-27 12.27

Time — Displays times in one of the following formats:

1-hh:mm:ss AM/PM format	12:24:55 AM
2-hh:mm AM/PM format	12:24 AM
3-Long International format	13:20:33
4-Short International format	14:55

Format	Description	Example
Text	Displays formulas instead of values.	+C7–C8
Hidden	Hides the cell contents.	
Reset	Resets all cells to the global setting (default).	

To set the format for a cell or block of cells, use the following steps:

1. Move the cell selector to the cell you want to format.

2. Select the Style pull-down menu.

3. Select the Numeric Format option. The Numeric Format submenu appears, as shown in Figure 13-1.

4. Select a format and press Enter.

5. To set the format for a single cell, press Enter. To format a block of cells, use the direction keys or the mouse to highlight the block and press Enter.

Shortcut Press Ctrl+F to access the Numeric Format submenu quickly.

Changing Fonts

You can modify the font you want Quattro Pro to print for a cell or a block of cells. In WYSIWYG mode, Quattro Pro displays the font you have selected for each cell.

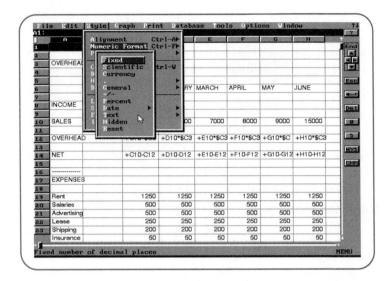

Figure 13-1. The Numeric Format submenu.

To modify a font for a cell or block of cells:

1. Move the cell selector to the cell where you want to begin modifying the font.

2. Select the Style pull-down menu.

3. Select the Font option. Quattro Pro displays a list of available fonts, as shown in Figure 13-2.

4. Select the font you want to use and press Enter.

5. Use the direction keys to extend the highlight over the cells you want to modify.

6. Press Enter. Figure 13-3 shows a worksheet with the cells in row 3 reformatted in bitstream Dutch 18 point font.

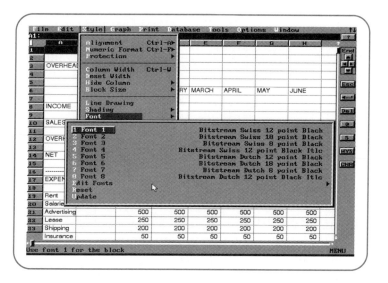

Figure 13-2. *The available fonts window.*

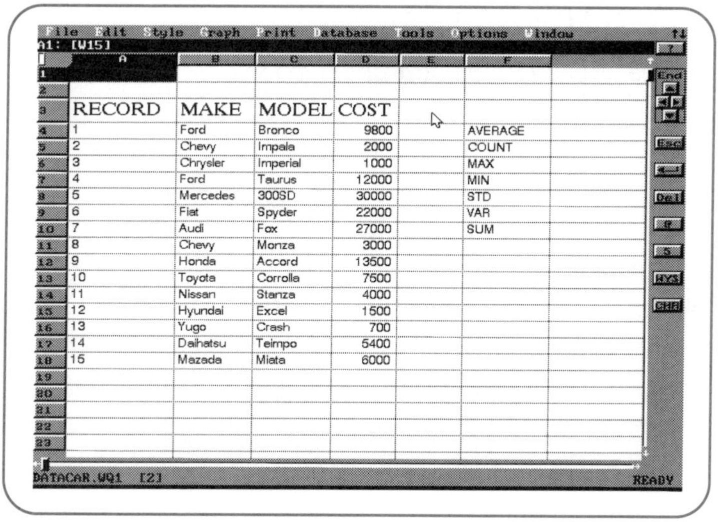

Figure 13-3. *A worksheet with the cells in row 3 reformatted in the bitstream Dutch 18 point font.*

If You Can't See Your Changes If you do not have the hardware to see the effect of modifying the font style, open the Print pull-down menu, select the Destination option and Screen Preview as the destination. Quattro Pro then displays the way the printed output will look on-screen.

Setting Global Formats

You can set the cell format, label alignment, and width of columns for the entire worksheet. After you set global options, you can override them by specifying other formatting options for individual cells or cell blocks, as described earlier.

To set a global format:

1. Select the Options pull-down menu.

2. Select the Formats option.

3. Select the option you want to set and press Enter.

4. Press Esc.

5. Select the Update option from the Options pull-down menu. The option you have selected is in effect for all current and future worksheets.

Protecting Cells

Quattro Pro's cell protection feature makes it impossible for you to make an entry in a cell designated as protected.

You can use the protection feature in two ways. You can protect the worksheet globally and set it to Disable, which allows you to edit all cells. Or you can protect single cells or cell blocks.

To protect a cell or cells from editing:

1. Select the Options pull-down menu.

2. Select the Protection option.

3. Select the Enable option. Quattro Pro returns you to the worksheet. All cells are now protected and cannot be edited.

4. Move the cell selector to the first cell that you do not want protected.

5. Select the Style pull-down menu.

6. Select the Protection option.

7. From the Protection submenu, select the Unprotect option. Quattro Pro returns you to the worksheet. To Unprotect a single cell, press Enter. To Unprotect a block of cells, use the direction keys to extend the cell selector, and then press Enter.

In this lesson you learned how to change the cell format, select a font for a block of cells, protect specific cells and set the format for all cells. In the next lesson you will learn how to use other enhancements to improve the appearance of your worksheets.

Lesson 14
Special Worksheet Effects

In this lesson you'll learn how to insert a page break, hide specific columns, add shading and lines to cells and freeze titles.

Inserting a Page Break

When you print a worksheet, Quattro Pro begins at the first cell in the upper left corner of the block you selected to print. Quattro Pro then calculates the space available on the paper which you specified for the printout. If the block is too large to fit on a single page, Quattro Pro prints a portion to a second page. (Lesson 15 explains how to print a worksheet.)

The place where Quattro Pro makes the page break may not be where you want it to be. To force a horizontal page break, use the following steps:

1. Move the cell selector to the cell where you want the page break to occur.

2. Select the Style pull-down menu.

3. Select the Insert Break option. A pair of colons appears in the cell. To remove the page break, move the cell selector to the cell and press Del.

Hiding Columns

Quattro Pro allows you to hide worksheet columns. When the columns are hidden, all calculations referencing the hidden cells remain valid. To hide a column or columns, use the following steps:

1. Move the cell selector to the column that you want to hide.

2. Select the Style pull-down menu.

3. Select the Hide Column option.

4. From the Hide Column submenu, select Hide. Quattro Pro returns you to the worksheet. To hide a single column, press Enter. To hide several columns, press the .(period) to anchor the cell selector, and use the direction keys or drag the mouse to expand the cell selector, then press Enter.

The columns are now hidden from view. In Figure 14-1, columns C through G are hidden. Note that the column letters are out of sequence.

Revealing Hidden Columns To reveal hidden columns, use the procedure for hiding columns but select the Expose option instead of Hide. Hidden columns have an asterick next to the column, for example, A* or B*. Click on each column or press . (period) and extend the highlight until you have selected all the columns you want to expose and press Enter.

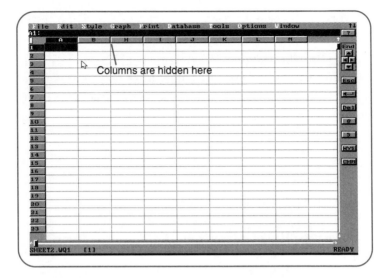

Figure 14-1. *A worksheet with columns C throught G hidden.*

Adding Shading to Cells

You can shade a block of cells with either gray or black scaling. The shaded cells appear in reverse video (on a black and white system) or in a distinct color. Use shading to emphasize selected worksheet cells.

To add shading to one or more cells, use the following steps:

1. Move the cell selector to the cell where you want the shading to begin.

2. Select the Style pull-down menu.

3. Select the Shading option.

4. Choose the Black or Grey option. Quattro Pro returns you to the worksheet. To select a single cell, press Enter. To select a block of cells, use the direction keys or drag the mouse to expand the cell selector and press Enter. Figure 14-2 shows a worksheet with a shaded cell block.

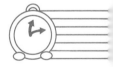

Figure 14-2. *Shaded cells in a worksheet.*

Removing Shading To remove the shading, follow the steps for shading but select None at the Shading option, and select the cells with shading.

Adding Lines

You can also emphasize areas of the worksheet by addng lines and borders. These lines will print with the worksheet. To add lines to a cell or cell block, use the following steps:

1. Move the cell selector to the first cell where you want to add lines.

2. Select the Style pull-down menu.

3. Select the Line Drawing option. Quattro Pro returns you to the worksheet. To add lines to a single cell, press Enter. Use the direction keys to extend the cell selector and select a block of cells, then press Enter.

4. The Placement dialog box appears, as shown in Figure 14-3. Select the appropriate option and press Enter.

5. The Line Types dialog box appears. Select the type of line you want and press Enter. Quattro Pro inserts the line choice you have made, and leaves the Placement dialog box open, allowing you to make changes.

6. Select Quit.

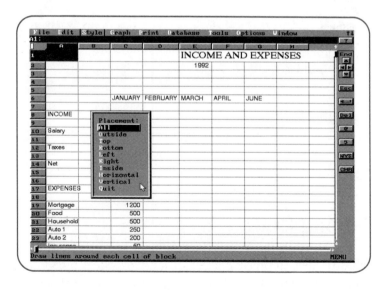

Figure 14-3. The Placement dialog box.

Freezing Titles

An optional way of seeing column and row labels without splitting the worksheet window into horizontal or vertical panes is to use the Locked Titles option. To lock row or column titles so that they appear on-screen at all times, no matter where you scroll in the worksheet, use the following steps:

1. Move the cell selector to the cell that is to the right of the row labels or below the column labels that you want to lock.

2. Select the Window pull-down menu.

3. Select Options.

4. From the Options submenu, select the Locked Titles option.

5. From the Locked Titles submenu, select the Horizontal or Vertical option (or Both) and press Enter. Selecting Horizontal locks the column titles. Selecting Vertical locks the row titles. Selecting the Both option locks both column and row titles.

   Unlocking Titles To unlock the titles, follow the steps for locking titles but select the Clear option from the Locking Titles submenu.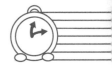

In this lesson you learned how to add a page break, hide a column, add shading and lines to cells and freeze row or column titles. In the next lesson you will learn how to print your worksheet.

Lesson 15
Printing a Worksheet

In this lesson you'll learn how to print your worksheet.

Selecting a Printer

When you installed Quattro Pro, you selected a printer to use with the program. However, at some point you may want to use a different printer. Quattro Pro allows you to select a new printer without going through the installation process. Use the following steps to specify a new printer:

1. Select the Options pull-down menu.

2. Select the Hardware option.

3. From the Hardware submenu, select the Printers option.

4. From the Printers submenu select the 1st Printer option.

5. From the 1st Printer submenu select the Type of Printer option. A list of printer manufacturers appears, as shown in Figure 15-1.

6. Use ↑ and ↓ to select the name of the printer manufacturer you want, and press Enter. If the company makes several printers, a submenu appears listing the models. Select the model name of your printer, and press Enter. Many printers have different printing modes. If

Quattro Pro displays a Mode submenu, select the mode you want and press Enter.

7. Quattro Pro returns you to the Type of Printer menu. If the printer you want to use requires additional settings, select them from this menu.

8. Select Quit three times.

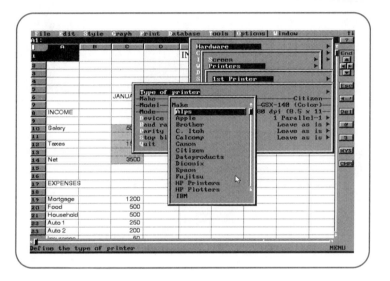

Figure 15-1. *A list of printer manufacturers.*

Selecting Print Options

Quattro Pro offers multiple options for printing. Figure 15-2 shows the Print pull-down menu. Table 15-1 describes each Print menu option.

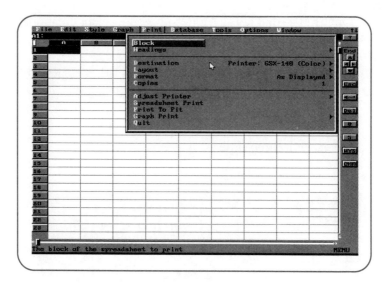

Figure 15-2. The Print pull-down menu.

Table 15-1. The Print menu options.

Option	Use to...
Block	Tell Quattro Pro which block of cells you want to print.
Headings	Print a Left heading or Top heading on every page.
Destination	Print to a printer, a file, a binary file, and a graphics printer or to see a Screen Preview mode.
Layout	Include headers or footers, enable Quattro Pro page breaks, set a percent scaling, set the page margins, measure the margins in characters lines or centimeters, determine the print orientation, enter a setup string, or reset the print options.

Option	Use to...
Format	Print the worksheet as it is displayed or print the cell contents (that is the formulas instead of the results of the formulas).
Copies	Print multiple copies of the worksheet.
Adjust Printer	Line up the print head with the paper.
Spreadsheet Print	Begin printing.
Print To Fit	Adjust the print block so that it fits on a single page.
Graph Print	Print a graph.

Seeing in Print Preview Mode

Before printing your worksheet to paper, you can see the worksheet as it will appear, using Quattro Pro's Screen Preview option. Previewing your printout is a good idea if you have inserted page breaks, or used special fonts or other enhancements. To preview a worksheet printout, use the following steps:

1. Select the Print pull-down menu.

2. Select the Block option and designate the block of cells to print.

3. Select the Destination option.

4. From the Destination submenu, select Screen Preview. You are returned to the Print pull-down menu.

5. Select the Spreadsheet Print option. Quattro Pro displays a preview version of the worksheet, like the one in Figure 15-3. To see an area of the worksheet in high detail, use the Zoom menu.

6. To return to the worksheet, press Esc.

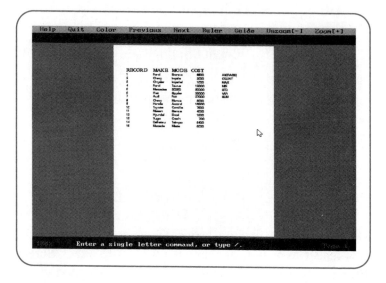

Figure 15-3. *A worksheet displayed in Screen Preview.*

Printing a Hard Copy of Your Worksheet

Quattro Pro offers several options for printing a hard copy of your worksheet, as outlined at the beginning of this lesson. To print a worksheet, use the following steps:

1. Select the Print pull-down menu.

2. Select a block of cells to print. If the cell selector is not at the beginning cell that you want to print, press Esc. Move the cell selector to the upper left cell in the print block. Press the . (period) to anchor the cell selector, and use the direction keys to expand the cell selector to the bottom right cell of the print block.

3. Press Enter. Quattro Pro returns you to the Print pull-down menu.

4. Select the Destination option. If you are using any special fonts, Print Orientation is Landscape or Banner, or you are using Percent Scaling or Print to Fit, you must select the Graphics Printer option. Otherwise, select Printer.

5. Select the Spreadsheet Print option. Quattro Pro prints your worksheet.

In this lesson you learned how to setup a printer, setup the print options, use printing a Print Preview and print a hard copy of your worksheet. In the next lesson you will learn how to produce enhanced printouts with Quattro Pro.

Enhanced Printouts

In this lesson you'll learn how to add headings to the pages of your printed worksheet, and headers and footers.

Printing with Headings

When you create a worksheet, it is normal that you have column and row labels. However, when you print your worksheet, the labels print only on the first page. So, any subsequent pages of the printed worksheet are simply rows and columns of numbers, making it difficult to match the values with their respective labels. To print the column headings on every page, use the following steps:

1. Select the Print pull-down menu.

2. Select the Headings option. Quattro Pro displays the Headings submenu shown in Figure 16-1.

3. From the Headings submenu, select the Top Heading option. Quattro Pro returns you to the worksheet.

4. Move the cell selector to the cell furthest left in the block that you want to print on each page.

5. Press . (period) to anchor the cell selector.

6. Use ← and → to expand the cell selector across the worksheet to select the column headings.

7. Press Enter. Quattro Pro enters the cell block into the Headings submenu. When you print the spreadsheet, the column headings selected print across the top of every page.

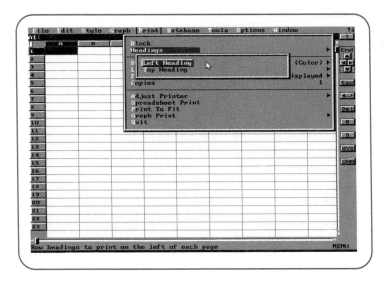

Figure 16-1. The Headings submenu.

Printing a Left Heading To print the row headings at the left edge of every page, follow the steps for printing column headings. Choose Left Heading from the Headings submenu, and select the cells from top to bottom that you want to print on every page.

Adding Headers and Footers

You can create headers and footers using the menus of Quattro Pro, rather than entering them in a cell like column and row headings. Headers and footers print on every page of the worksheet, and usually include information like the worksheet title. To add a header or footer to a worksheet printout, use the following steps:

1. Select the Print pull-down menu.

2. Select the Layout option.

3. From the Layout submenu, select Header or Footer. The Header or Footer dialog box appears, as shown in Figure 16-2.

4. Type the text or values that you want.

5. Press Enter. The beginning of the header or footer displays in the submenu.

6. Select Quit twice.

Removing a Header or Footer To remove a header or footer, follow the steps to create a header or footer but at the header or footer dialog box, use Backspace to erase the entry. Press Enter.

Printing Page Numbers and Dates To print a page number simply enter the # (number sign) in the header or footer. An @ (at sign) entered into the header or footer prints the current system date.

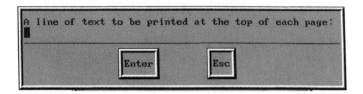

Figure 16-2. The Header dialog box.

In this lesson you will learn how to print the column and row labels on every page of the worksheet, and how to add running headers and footers. In the next lesson you will learn how to create graphs of your worksheet data.

Lesson 17
Creating Graphs

In this lesson you'll learn how to select a block of cells to graph, and select different kinds of graphs.

Quattro Pro Graphs

With Quattro Pro, you can create 10 types of two-dimensional graphs and four types of three-dimensional graphs. Following are descriptions of Quattro Pro's graph types:

Line	A line graph is a line or lines that reflect a series of numbers, usually over time
Bar	A bar graph is a series of bars, the height of each bar is determined by the value it represents
XY	An XY-graph uses lines to plot the relationship between two values
Stacked Bar	The stacked bar graph combines values in a stacked bar; each piece of the bar represents a specific series

Pie Chart   A pie chart is used to graph a single series; each slice of pie represents its relationship to the whole pie

Area   An area graph is a line graph that is filled in underneath the line

Rotated Bar   A rotated bar graph takes the bar graph and rotates it 90 degrees so that the bars run horizontally across the page

Column   A column graph is a variation of the pie graph in that the column is a single series of values

High-Low-Close   A High-Low-Close graph is used to plot three stock price values on a single point in time, the high price, the low price, and the closing price

Text   A text graph is not a graph, but a drawing area; the Graph Annotator is used to create the output

Three-dimensional graphs are plotted the same as two-dimensional graphs. The difference is that Quattro Pro displays the graph in a three-dimensional perspective.

Bar   A three-dimensional bar graph resembles a two-dimensional graph except that the bars appear on a three-dimensional grid

Step   The step graph is similar to the bar graph except that the bars of a series touch

Ribbon   A ribbon graph is essentially a line graph with the lines widened into a segmented ribbon

Area   An area graph is a line graph that is filled in on a three dimensional grid

Selecting the Cells to Graph

To create a graph, you first must select the cells that contain the values you want to graph. This is called selecting the graph series. You can plot up to six different series of values in a single graph. You can also plot an *X-axis series*.

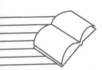
X-Axis Series The X-Axis series is used to add labels to the horizontal axis of the graph. Follow the same steps used for plotting values.

To select a series to graph, follow these steps:

1. Select the Graph pull-down menu.

2. Select the Series option. Quattro Pro displays the Series submenu shown in Figure 17-1.

3. From the Series submenu, select the 1st series option and press Enter. Quattro Pro takes you back into the worksheet.

4. Move the cell selector to the first cell containing a value you want to plot.

5. Press **.** (period) to anchor the cell selector.

6. Use the direction keys to expand the cell selector across the cells in the series.

7. Press Enter. Quattro Pro returns you to the Series submenu. If you want to plot more than one series, repeat steps 3 through 7 for each series.

8. To see the graph, press F10. To return to the worksheet, press Esc.

Fast Graph To create a basic graph in a hurry, select the Fast Graph option from the Graph pull-down menu (or press Ctrl+G), specify the series to graph, and press Enter.

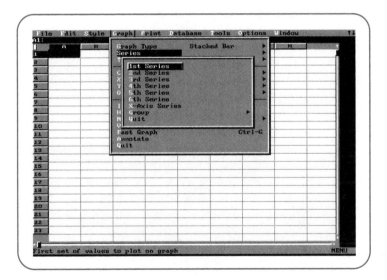

Figure 17-1. The Series submenu.

Choosing a Graph Type

Quattro Pro offers a wide variety of graphs. Experiment with the graph types to find the best representation of your worksheet because not every graph type is appropriate for every data set.

1. Select the Graph pull-down menu.

2. Select the Graph Type option. In WYSIWYG mode, Quattro Pro displays the graph types shown in Figure 17-2. In character mode, the Graph Type submenu displays a list of graph types.

3. Select the graph type you want.

4. Press Enter.

5. Select the View option from the Graph pull-down menu or press F10.

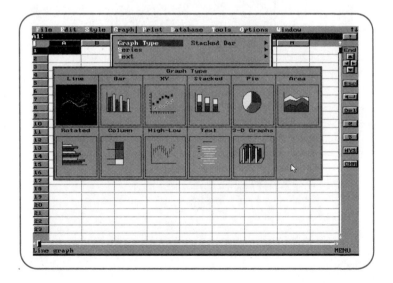

Figure 17-2. The graph types.

The data in the series is now displayed in the graph style you selected. To try a different graph type, press Esc to go back to the Graph pull-down menu and repeat the steps outlined previously.

Adding Graph Titles and Legends

After you select the graph type you want, you can add a two-line title to the top of the graph and legends that detail what each plot represents. Figure 17-3 shows a bar graph with titles and legend added. To add a title to a graph, use the following steps:

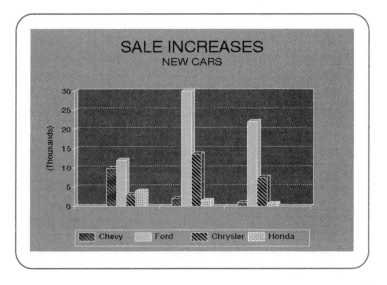

Figure 17-3. *A bar graph with titles and lengend added.*

1. Select the Graph pull-down menu.

2. Select the Text option.

3. From the Text submenu select the 1st Line option.

4. In the 1st Line dialog box, type the text of the first line of the title.

5. Press Enter. If you want to add a second line, select that option and type a second line of text.

6. Press F10 to see the graph with your changes.

7. Using the steps above, add a line of text to the horizontal X-axis and the vertical Y-axis.

Adding Legends

A graph legend aids in identifying the meaning of the colors, markers or patterns in the graph. To add a legend to a graph, use the following steps:

1. Select the Graph pull-down menu.

2. Select the Text option.

3. From the Text submenu, select the Legends option.

4. Select the series for which you want to create a legend.

5. Type the text for the legend. (You cannot use a cell reference.)

6. Press Enter.

7. Press F10 to see the graph with the legend.

8. To add more legends, follow steps 4-7 as described above.

Saving Graphs

To save a graph, you must give it a unique name. The graph is stored as part of the worksheet. The values in the graph are interactive with the worksheet, so if you change the worksheet values upon which the graph is based, the graph changes. If you create more than one graph for a worksheet, remember to add a unique name to each. To save a graph, use the following steps:

1. Select the Graph pull-down menu.

2. Select the Name option.

3. From the Name submenu, select the Create option. The Create dialog box appears.

4. Type the name of the graph, which can be up to 15 characters in length.

5. Press Enter.

Retrieving a Saved Graph

If you have saved more than one graph with a worksheet, you must follow these steps to retrieve it:

1. Select the Graph pull-down menu.

2. Select the Name option.

3. From the Name submenu, select the Display option. A list of all the graphs stored is displayed.

4. Select the name of the graph you want to see, and press Enter.

Lesson 18

Enhancing and Printing Graphs

In this lesson you'll learn how to add enhancements and print your graphs.

Adding Graph Enhancements

Virtually every aspect of a Quattro Pro graph can be enhanced in some way. The options for customizing a graph series appear on the Customize Series submenu. Table 18-1 describes the options in this submenu.

Table 18-1. The Customize Series submenu options.

Option	Use to
Colors	Change the colors used to display individual series.
Fill patterns	Change the patterns used to fill bars or area graph sections.
Markers and Lines	Change the type of marker that plots a point or the type of line that connects the plotted points.
Bar Width	Adjust the width of the bar in a bar graph.

Option	Use to
Interior Labels	On a bar chart, you can add a label inside the graph above each individual bar.
Override Type	Mix a bar chart with a line chart.
Y-axis	Add a second Y-axis on the right side of the chart.
Pies	Modify the label format, explode a piece of pie, change the fill patterns for each slice of pie or add or remove tick marks from the pie to its respective label.
Update	Make the current graph customization the defaults.
Reset	Make the graph customizations the Quattro Pro defaults.

Displaying the Current Graph Pressing F10, when working in the worksheet, displays the current graph.

After you have created or retrieved a graph, you can customize each series plotted as follows:

1. Select the Graph pull-down menu.

2. Select the Customize Series option. The Customize Series submenu appears, as shown in Figure 18-1.

111

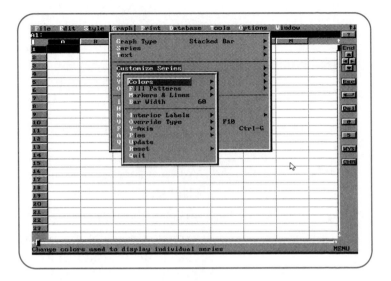

***Figure 18-1.** The Customize Series submenu.*

Customizing the X- and Y-Axes

The Graph pull-down menu offers six options to modify the display of the X- and Y-axes. The X- and Y-axes can be modified as you create the graph or by retrieving a saved graph and making the changes. When you select the X-axis or Y-axis, the following options appear:

Scale	Select automatic or manual; if you select manual, you need to make an entry in the low, high, and increment settings
Low	Enter the minimum value that you want plotted
High	Enter the maximum value you want plotted

Increment	Enter the amount to increment on the axis
Format of Ticks	Select the type of value and the display mode
# of Minor Ticks	If the axis labels are too crowded, you can use this option to delete a portion of the ticks
Display Scaling	Quattro Pro automatically scales each axis to fit the series assigned to it, and adds the definition of the numbers in thousands, millions etc.
Mode	Values can be scaled in normal or logarithmic mode

To modify either axis, follow the steps below:

1. Select the Graph pull-down menu.

2. Select the X-axis or Y-axis option. If you select the X-axis, the X-axis submenu appears, as shown in Figure 18-2.

3. If you want to have the scaling set to your specifications, change the Scale option from Automatic to Manual.

4. After making your changes, press F10 to see the effect.

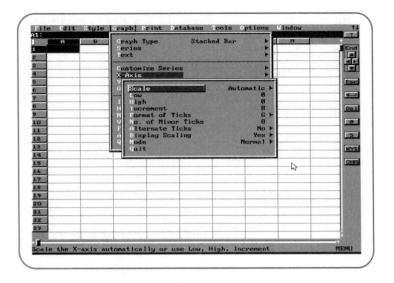

Figure 18-2. *The X-Axis series submenu.*

Accessing the Graph Annotator

The Graph Annotator is a built in graph editing environment. After you have created a graph, the Annotator can add many things that normally are only found in graphics packages. Following is a list of items available with the Graph Annotator:

- Boxed Text

- Arrows

- Straight lines

- Curved lines

- Polygons

- Squares

- Rectangles

- Ellipses

- Links to graph series

  To access the Graph Annotator, use the following steps:

1. Select the Graph pull-down menu.

2. Press / (forward slash). The Annotator screen appears, as shown in Figure 18-3.

3. Select the type of enhancements you want from the icons at the top of the Annotator screen. You can do this by clicking on them with the mouse or by selecting the letter keys matching the icons with the keyboard.

4. Press / (forward slash) and Q to exit the Annotator.

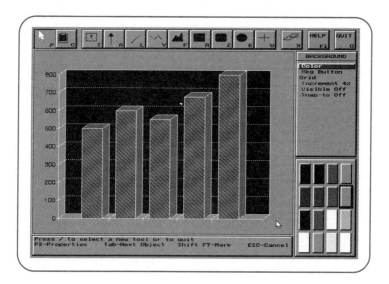

Figure 18-3. The Annotator screen.

115

Printing a Graph

Follow these steps to print the graph currently on-screen (if you don't have a graph currently on-screen, retrieve a saved graph before using the following steps):

1. Select the Print pull-down menu.

2. Select the Graph Print option.

3. From the Graph Print submenu, select the Destination option.

4. Select Graphics printer as the destination.

5. If you want to print the current graph (the one you see if you press F10) select Go. If you want to print a different graph, select the Name option and then select the name of the graph to make current, and press Enter. Then select Go.

In this lesson you learned how to enhance aspects of a graph, access the Annotator and print a graph. In the next lesson you will learn how to use Quattro Pro databases.

Lesson 19
Creating a Simple Database

In this lesson you'll learn how to create and save a database.

Database Basics

Quattro Pro can store, sort, and retrieve information entered as a *database*. A database is a collection of information that has a common link. For example, if you wanted to save the names and addresses of all the people on your holiday card list, you would save the same pieces of information for each person; first name, last name, street number and so on. Each piece of information is entered into a separate *field*. All of the fields for each person on the list make a *record*. In Quattro Pro, each record is entered into a separate row, and the fields appear in columns. Figure 19-1 shows a database and its component parts.

You must observe the following rules when you enter database information:

- **Field Names**: The first row in the database must be field names, for example, FNAME for first name, LNAME for the last name. The field names cannot be longer than 15 characters, and cannot contain any of the following operators: +, −, *, /, or ^. A field name cannot be in use elsewhere on the worksheet, as a block name or as a field. Do not skip a row between the field names row and the first record.

- **Records**: Records cannot have any spaces between the rows. The data in each field (column) must be of the same type. For example, zip codes must all be in the same field. You can create a calculated field; one that uses information from another field of the same record and produces a result. (To do so, enter a formula, as explained in Lesson 9.)

Field Names Row   A Single Record

RECORD	FNAME	LNAME	NUMBER	STREET	CITY	STATE
1	Kathy	Walters	334	Elm	Myrtle	MO
2	Dave	Tetzlaff	20998	Lenuestra	Ramona	CA
3	Edgar	Winter	333	N. Main	Hopkins	KY
4	Henry	Late	1313	Bird Ln.	Poway	CA
5	Charles	Erkle	RR 1	Box 46	Le Center	MN
6	Gloria	Strong	13141	Lenares	Lac Battle	MN
7	Alexander	Grape	1415	Turtle	Boise	ID
8	William	Lobo	50098	Rose	Del Mar	CA
9	Char	Burger	9008	Pasture	Queso	CA
10	Cathy	Carter	7654	Goober	Plains	GA
11	Bob	Kelly	777	Ironwood	Disk	MN
12	Rona	Fowler	4545	Mt. High	Waco	TX
13	Scott	Wulf	67000	The Peak	St. George	UT
14	Cyrus	Gladrock	1101	Serpt	Solana	CA
15	Trevor	Kong	33009	King	New York	NY
16	Scott	Lona	10922	Quest	San Diego	CA
17	Pearl	Braun	9987	Ageis	Le Center	MN
18	Rebecca	Liver	77765	Body	Mony	CA
19	Larry	Groung	30009	Time	Western	MT

Database Area

Fields

Figure 19-1. A database and its components.

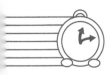

Record Numbering It is a good idea to add a column that numbers the records so if the records are sorted incorrectly, you can use the numbered column to restore the records to their original order.

Creating a Database

Quattro Pro databases are created in table format. Columns are used as fields and rows are used to hold individual records. The top row of the database contains the field names. The rows below the field names contain the records. You enter the information, labels or numbers, as you usually would. If you want to enter street numbers with the street names, start the entry with an apostrophe so that Quattro Pro interprets the entry as a label.

To activate the database, after you have entered the field labels and the records, use the following steps:

1. Select the Database pull-down menu and select the Query option. (The next lesson tells you more about the Query menu.)

2. From the Query submenu, select the Block option. Quattro Pro prompts you for a block of cells to define the database. Include the row with the field names.

3. Select the Assign Names option. When you do, Quattro Pro assigns block names to each field column using the top row entry as the block name.

Adding Records

To add records to the database, enter the information at the bottom or end of the current records. Remember to change the block addresses assigned to the database area block names after adding records or any actions you perform will not be accurate. Also, select the Database pull-down menu, the Query option, the Block option, and the Assign Names command to redefine the field cell blocks.

Adding Columns

If you add more columns of information, you are adding additional fields. Remember to redefine the database block and to select the Assign Names command to make the block names correct.

Saving the Database

After you've entered data and named the database cell block, save the database as you would any other worksheet file. It is a good idea to save worksheets that contain databases in a separate directory. (For more information on working with directories, see the DOS Primer in the back of this book.)

Assigning a Block Name to the Database

After you have entered the records, you can select the block of rows and columns that contain the records, and give the block a name. That way, if you want to perform a sort, you can use the block name instead of the cell addresses to define the sort. Remember, if you add records after creating the block name, you must rename the block to include the added records.

In this lesson you learned how to use the basic components and structure of a database. In the next lesson you will learn how to search and sort a database.

Lesson 20
Searching and Sorting a Database

In this lesson you will learn how to sort your database, using one or two sort keys, and construct a criteria table for locating specific records.

Sorting a Database

When you sort a database, the key thing to remember is not to include the top row—the one with the field names—in the block of cells to sort. Quattro Pro sorts by using the information in one to five columns. The column(s) on which Quattro Pro bases its sort is called a *sort key*. For example, sorting by the LNAME field is a common operation. However, before you sort a database, you must activate the database by selecting the Database pull-down menu, the Query option, the Block option, and the Assign Names command. Or simply type in the name of the database cell block (see Lesson 19) and press Enter.

To sort a database using one sort key, use the following steps:

1. Select the Database pull-down menu.

2. Select the Sort option.

3. From the Sort submenu, select the Block option. Quattro Pro takes you back to the worksheet. Move the cell

selector to the upper left cell in the block that you want to sort. Press . (period) to anchor the cell selector, and use the direction keys to expand the cell selector over the entire block of cells. (Don't include the field names!)

4. Press Enter. You are returned to the Sort submenu.

5. Select the 1st key option. Quattro Pro returns you to the worksheet. Move the cell selector to the field column that you want to sort the records by, or type in the name of the field column from the field names row if you've used the the Database pull-down menu, the Query option, the Block option and the Assign Names command previously.

6. Press Enter. Quattro Pro displays the Sort Order dialog box.

7. Select either D for descending, or A for Ascending. Descending order sorts the records from the highest value to the lowest. For example, if the column contains the LNAME entries, all names beginning with W are moved to the top of the column.

8. Select Go. Figure 20-1 shows an example of a database sorted by the LNAME field.

Sorting with Two Keys

In the preceding example, a database was sorted based on a single field column. Many times a database contains records that are identical in the 1st key field column. So, to break ties, Quattro Pro can create secondary sorts on as many as four other columns.

To sort by more than one key, follow the steps for a one-key sort through step 5. When the Sort submenu appears, select the 2nd key option and select a second field column on which to base a sort. You can also specify a 3rd, 4th, or 5th key. Press Enter.

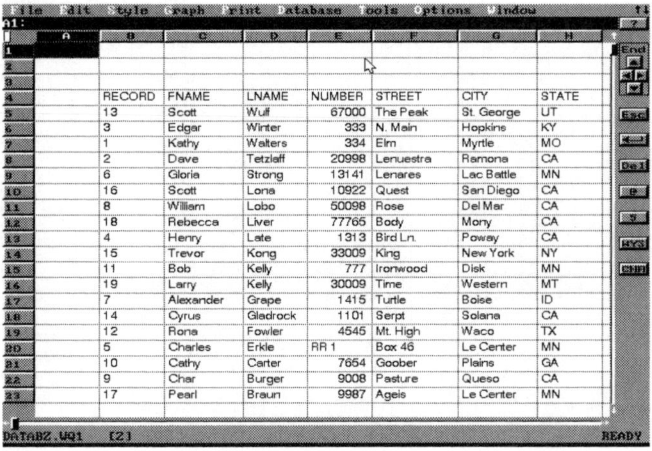

RECORD	FNAME	LNAME	NUMBER	STREET	CITY	STATE
13	Scott	Wulf	67000	The Peak	St. George	UT
3	Edgar	Winter	333	N. Main	Hopkins	KY
1	Kathy	Walters	334	Elm	Myrtle	MO
2	Dave	Tetzlaff	20998	Lenuestra	Ramona	CA
6	Gloria	Strong	13141	Lenares	Lac Battle	MN
16	Scott	Lona	10922	Quest	San Diego	CA
8	William	Lobo	50098	Rose	Del Mar	CA
18	Rebecca	Liver	77765	Body	Mony	CA
4	Henry	Late	1313	Bird Ln.	Poway	CA
15	Trevor	Kong	33009	King	New York	NY
11	Bob	Kelly	777	Ironwood	Disk	MN
19	Larry	Kelly	30009	Time	Western	MT
7	Alexander	Grape	1415	Turtle	Boise	ID
14	Cyrus	Gladrock	1101	Serpt	Solana	CA
12	Rona	Fowler	4545	Mt. High	Waco	TX
5	Charles	Erkle	RR 1	Box 46	Le Center	MN
10	Cathy	Carter	7654	Goober	Plains	GA
9	Char	Burger	9008	Pasture	Queso	CA
17	Pearl	Braun	9987	Ageis	Le Center	MN

Figure 20-1. A database sorted by the LNAME field.

If Quattro Pro encounters two records with identical entries in the 1st sort key field column, it checks the 2nd sort key field column to determine how to order the two records, and so on. Figure 20-2 shows a database sorted by LNAME and STATE.

Modifying Sort Rules

With some databases, the standard rules for sorting are not useful. For example, if the field column you selected as the 1st sort key has both label and value entries, Quattro Pro automatically places the 1st sort key records at the bottom of the database.

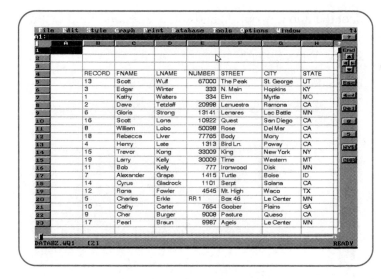

Figure 20-2. *A database sorted by LNAME and STATE.*

To modify the sort order, use these steps:

1. Select the Database pull-down menu.

2. Select the Sort Rules option.

   The Sort Rules submenu opens, giving the following options:

Numbers before Labels	Select Yes if you want records that contain numbers to be positioned at the top of the list
Label Order	Select Dictionary if you want the labels in the column to sort Aa Bb; The ASCII order sorts all uppercase letters first, ABC etc.

3. Make the selections you want and press Enter.

124

4. Select Quit.

5. Select Go to resort the records.

Searching for Records

To search for records, you first have to create a *criteria table* that defines the search criteria. Position the criteria table below or to the side of your database. Then when you want to search a database, you must include the field names as part of the block of cells to search. The search options appear on the Database pull-down menu's Query submenu, and are described in Table 20-1.

Table 20-1. The Database Query submenu options.

Option	Use to
Block	Specify the block of cells in the database containing the records, including the field names.
Criteria Table	Specify a block of cells CONTAINING the field names and the search criteria.
Output Block	Specify a block of cells to which the records that you extract will be copied to.
Assign Names	Make the field names the criteria table names.
Locate	Locate records as specified in the criteria table.
Extract	Copy records meeting the criteria to the output block.

continued

125

Table 20-1. (continued)

Option	Use to
Unique	Extract only unique values that match a query criterion, no duplicate records.
Delete	Delete all records meeting criteria.
Reset	Change all of the criteria settings.

To initiate a search, follow these steps:

1. Select the Database pull-down menu.

2. Select the Query option. The Query submenu opens.

3. Select the Block option. Quattro Pro returns you to the worksheet. Enter the cell addresses that contain the records and the field names, or use the direction keys to extend the highlight over the cells.

4. Select the Assign Names option. Nothing happens on-screen, but the top row of the database becomes the block names for each column.

5. Next, create a criteria table at the bottom of the database. Copy the field names to a blank area of the worksheet. Move the cell pointer to the top row of the database (the field names row) and use the Copy command, from the Edit pull-down menu, to copy the top row of cells.

6. Position the cell pointer in a blank area below the database and copy the field names there. Enter the label CRITERIA above the copied field names.

7. The criteria table includes the rows of cells that you copied to the bottom of the database and the row directly beneath it. (You can include more blank rows in a criteria table if you plan to search for more than one entry in a field.) For example, if the field names are copied to row 40, row 41 is also part of the criteria table. Select the Criteria Table option from the Database pull-down menu's Query submenu, and enter the cell address of the copied field names and the row underneath to activate your criteria table.

8. To enter a search criteria, close the Database pull-down menu by pressing Esc. Move the cell pointer to the cell directly beneath the field name that you want to use in the query. For example, if you wanted to find a record by the Last Name entry, you would move the cell pointer to the cell under the LNAME field name and enter the name for which you are searching, such as SMITH. Figure 20-3 shows a database with a criteria table and search criteria.

9. Open the Database pull-down menu and select the Query option.

10. To find a record, select the Locate option. The cursor moves to the first record that meets the criteria. Press ↓ to move to the next record that matches the search criteria.

Extracting Records

If you want to Extract records from the database, you must first define an Output Block, using the Database pull-down menu and the Query options, where the records will be copied to. Usually the Output Block is several rows beneath the criteria table.

Remember, if you add records to the database, you must redefine the database block.

Criteria Table   Search criteria

Figure 20-3. *Database with a criteria table and search criteria.*

Printing a Database Report

Printing a datbase report is the same as printing a worksheet, although you probably will print a smaller portion of the worksheet. To print a database, follow these steps:

1. Select the Print pull-down menu.

2. Select the Block option. Specify the database block. If you extracted records and want to print them, designate the cells containing the output block.

3. Select the Spreadsheet Print option.

Lesson 21
Database Statistics

In this lesson you'll learn how to analyze values in database records.

Database Statistical Functions

Quattro Pro's statistical functions enable you to perform basic statistical operations on database values. Enter these functions in a cell, in a column other than the one with the values you want to analyze. The operations you can perform are listed below in the formula format:

@DAVG
(block,column,criteria)
Averages the entries in a numeric field; the criteria portion of the formula is optional, but if used, averages only the records specified by the criteria

@DCOUNT
(block,column,criteria)
Counts the number of entries in the specified field; the criteria portion of the formula is optional, but if used, counts only the records specified by the criteria

@DMAX **(block,column,criteria)**	Finds the largest value in the field; the criteria portion of the formula is optional, but if used, searches only the records specified by the criteria for the largest value
@DMIN **(block,column,criteria)**	Finds the smallest value in the field; the criteria portion of the formula is optional, but if used, searches only the records specified by the criteria for the smallest value
@DSTD **(block,column,criteria)**	Calculates the standard deviation of the values in the field; the criteria portion of the formula is optional, but if used, uses only the records specified by the criteria in the calculation
@DSUM **(block,column,criteria)**	Sums the entries in a numeric field; the criteria portion of the formula is optional, but if used, sums only the records specified by the criteria
@DVAR **(block,column,criteria)**	Calculates the variance of a numeric field; the criteria portion of the formula is optional, but if used, uses only the records specified by the criteria for the calculation

Figure 21-1 includes a database with the statistical functions used.

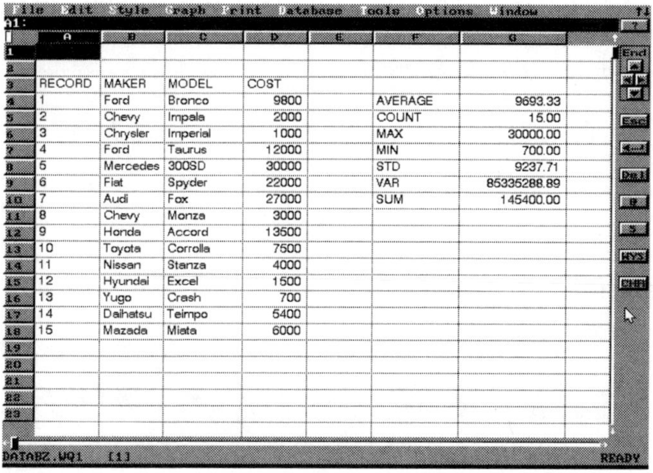

RECORD	MAKER	MODEL	COST			
1	Ford	Bronco	9800		AVERAGE	9693.33
2	Chevy	Impala	2000		COUNT	15.00
3	Chrysler	Imperial	1000		MAX	30000.00
4	Ford	Taurus	12000		MIN	700.00
5	Mercedes	300SD	30000		STD	9237.71
6	Fiat	Spyder	22000		VAR	85335288.89
7	Audi	Fox	27000		SUM	145400.00
8	Chevy	Monza	3000			
9	Honda	Accord	13500			
10	Toyota	Corrolla	7500			
11	Nissan	Stanza	4000			
12	Hyundai	Excel	1500			
13	Yugo	Crash	700			
14	Daihatsu	Telmpo	5400			
15	Mazada	Miata	6000			

Figure 21-1. The database statistical functions.

Database Statistical Formula Syntax

To create the statistical formula shown in Figure 21-1, move the cell pointer to the cell where you want the result to appear and type the function with the correct syntax. All of the database statistical functions use the following syntax:

```
@FUNCTION(block,column,criteria)
```

The *@FUNCTION* is the statistical function, such as @DSTD. The *block* includes all of the cells that contain all of the records and the field names in the database. *Column* is the column position of the database field on which to perform the calculation, (starting with zero as the leftmost column.) The *criteria* is an optional portion of the formula.

For example, by using the criteria portion of the formula, you can specify that only certain records in the database be considered in the calculation.

In the example database, shown in Figure 21-2, the block is A3..D18, the column is 3. The criteria is block D4..D18. Notice cell G4. The cell entry @DAVG(A3..D18, 3, D4..D18) averages the values in the third column of the database.

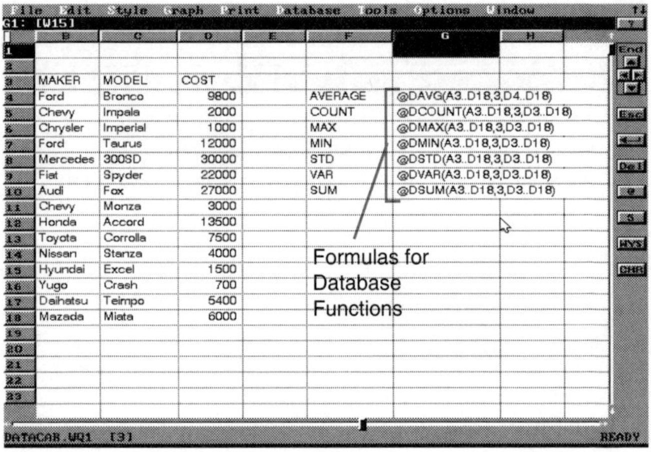

Figure 21-2. An example database.

In this lesson you learned how to use statistical functions on a database. In the next lesson you will learn how to specify program defaults.

Lesson 22
Setting Program Defaults

In this lesson you'll learn how to set the Quattro Pro program defaults.

Hardware Options

When you installed Quattro Pro, the program checked to determine the type of system hardware you have. It also helped you install the default printer. However, you may want to override the defaults and can do so using the Options pull-down menu and the Hardware option.

To change a default hardware setting, use the following steps:

1. Select the Options pull-down menu.

2. Select the Hardware option. The Hardware submenu appears as shown in Figure 22-1.

   Three options can be modified. Selecting the Screen option opens the Screen submenu with the options described below:

   Screen type   Select this option to override the screen type

   Resolution   Select this option to override the resolution

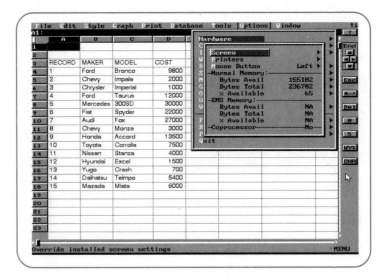

Figure 22-1. The Hardware submenu.

Aspect Ratio   Select this option to change the way circles are drawn on your computer screen; Quattro Pro displays a circle that can be modified to display as close to perfectly round as your screen allows

CGA Snow   Select this option if your system
Suppression   includes a CGA type monitor and lots of snow is visible; with this option, the screen display slows down

If you select the Printers option, a submenu appears with the following options:

1st Printer   Select this option to determine the make, model and capabilities of the printer you plan to use most of the time

2nd Printer	Select this option to determine the make, model and capabilities of an alternate printer
Default Printer	Select this option to switch between the two printers you have defined
Plotter Speed	Select this option to set the print speed of a plotter
Fonts	Select this option to use LaserJet font cartridges installed in the printer; this option includes a setting for autoscaling of fonts in relation to the graph size
Auto LF	Select this option if your printer keeps printer on a single line
Single Sheet	Select this option if your printer can print only a single sheet of paper at a time

If you select the Mouse Button option, the Mouse Button submenu with two choices appears: Right or Left. If you use your left hand to run your mouse, you may want to switch the active button to right. (To do this, refer to Lesson 2.)

3. Make your selections from any of the submenus. Press Enter to return to the Options pull-down menu.

4. After you make changes to any of the Hardware options, select the Update option from the Options pull-down menu to make the changes permanent.

135

Memory Information If you have installed more memory in your computer and want to see if Quattro Pro recognizes it, the Hardware submenu lists the amount of active memory. And if you have very large worksheets, you can check and see if you are in danger of running out of memory.

Font Options

Quattro Pro's print fonts can be modified. In a previous lesson, you selected a block of cells and modified the font. You may also modify the default font used by Quattro Pro.

To change the default font, use the following steps:

1. Select the Style pull-down menu.

2. Select the Font option. The fonts currently available are displayed.

3. Select the Edit Fonts option.

4. Select the font you wish to modify and press Enter. The Edit Fonts submenu appears, as shown in Figure 22-2. The typeface, the Point Size, the Style, and the Color can be modified. Select and change any of these options.

5. After making the changes you want, select the Update option from the Options pull-down menu to save the new settings as the defaults.

In this lesson you learned how to change the default hardware settings and modify the Font.

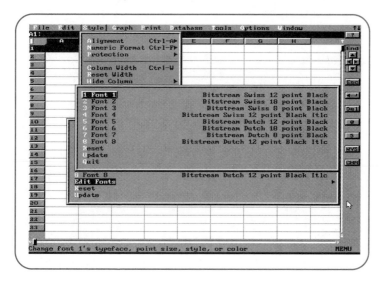

Figure 22-2. *The Edit Fonts submenu.*

With the end of this lesson, you have completed the *10 Minute Guide to Quattro Pro 3.0.* At the back of this book, you'll find a Table of Features, a Table of Functions, and a DOS Primer that will introduce you to several of the basic DOS commands.

Overtime

Appendix A
Table of Functions

As explained in Lesson 9, Quattro Pro includes hundreds of built-in functions that perform complex mathematical problems. For more informaton and a complete list of functions, refer to *The First Book of Quattro Pro, Revised Edition*. The most commonly used functions are described below:

Mathematical Functions

@ABS(X)	Calculates the absolute value of X
@RAND	Calculates a random number between 0 and 1
@ROUND(X,NUM)	Rounds the number X, to the number of digits specified by the num criterial
@SQRT(X	Calculates the square root of X

Statistical Functions

@AVG(list)	Calculates the average in the list; the list can consist of one block of cells, several blocks, or numbers

@COUNT(list)	Calculates the number of values in the list; the list can consist of one block of cells, several blocks, or numbers
@MAX(list)	Finds the largest value in the list; the list can consist of one block of cells, several blocks, or numbers
@MIN(list)	Finds the smallest value in the list; the list can consist of one block of cells, several blocks, or numbers
@SUM(list)	Calculates the total of the values in list; the list can consist of one block of cells, several blocks, or numbers

String Functions

@LOWER(string)	Changes the character in string to lowercase
@PROPER(string)	Changes the first letter in each of the words to uppercase
@REPEAT(string,num)	Repeats the string the number of times specified by number
@UPPER(string)	Changes the characters in the string to uppercase

139

Financial Functions

@CTERM
(interest,future,present)

Calculates the number of compounding periods needed to grow the present value to a future value

@DDB
(cost,salvage,life,period)

Calculates depreciation using the double declining balance method

@FV
(payments,interest,term)

Calculates the future value of an investment

@IRR(guess,block)

Calculates the internal rate of return

@NPER
(interest,payment,principal)

Calculates the number of periods needed to reach a target value

@NPV(interest,block)

Calculates the net present value of a series of cash flows

@PAYMNT
(interest,per,nper,principal)

Calculates the payment on a loan

@PV
(interest,periods,payment)

Calculates the present value of an annuity

@RATE
(future,present,term)

Calculates the interest rate needed to reach a future value

@SLN(cost,salvage,life)

Calculates depreciation using the straight line method

@SYD
(cost,salvage,life,period)

Calculates depreciation using the sum of the years' digit method

@TERM
(payments,interest,future)

Calculates the number of periods needed to reach a future value

Date and Time Functions

@DATE(year,month,day)

Converts the date into a serial number

@DAY(serial date)

Converts the serial number to a date

@HOUR(serial time)

Converts the serial time to a number

@MONTH(serial date)

Converts the serial date to a number

@TODAY

Displays the current date

@YEAR(serial date)

Converts the serial date to a number

Features Keys	Action	Description
F1	Help	Display the help screens
F2	Edit	Edit a cell entry
Shift-F2	Debug	Debugs macros
Alt-F2	Macro Menu	Displays the macro menu
F3	Choices	Lists block names
Shift-F3	Macros	Lists availabe macros
Alt-F3	Functions	Lists the functions
F4	Absolute Value	Makes cell addresess absolute
F5	Goto	Moves cell selector to designated cell
Shift-F5	Window Select	Lists open windows
Alt-F5	Undo	Reverses previous action (fist select /Optons Other Undo Enable)
F6	Pane	Moves the cell selector to next open pane

Features Keys	Action	Description
Shift-F6	Next Window	Moves the cell selector to next open window
Alt-F6	Zoom Window	Expands current window to full screen
F7	Query	Executes previous query
Shift-F7	Select	Selects a block
Alt-F7	All Select	Selects or deselects all files in the File Manager
F8	Table	Repeats the last what-if command
Shift-F8	Move	In the File Manager it moves the selected files to the clipboard
F9	Calc	Recalcualtes the spreadsheet
Shift-F9	Copy	In the File Manager it copies the the files selected in the active file list and stores them in the clipboard
F10	Graph	Displays the current graph
Shift-F10	Copy	In the File Manager it inserts any files stored on the clipboard into the directory displayed in the active file list

This section explains some of the DOS procedures you will need while using Quattro Pro 3.0.

DOS is your computer's Disk Operating System. It functions as a go-between program, connecting the various components of your computer system with one another. The following sections explain how to use DOS on your computer.

Changing Disk Drives

Once DOS is loaded, you should see a *prompt* (also known as the DOS prompt) on-screen that appears in one of two ways: A:> or A> (or C:> or B:>). This prompt tells you which disk drive is currently active. The hard disk drive is usually labeled C. The floppy disk drives are usually labeled drives A and B. If you have only one floppy drive, it's usually A and you have no drive B. You can activate a different drive at any time by performing the following steps:

1. Make sure there's a formatted disk in the drive you want to activate.

2. Type the letter of the drive followed by a colon. For example, type A: .

3. Press Enter. The DOS prompt changes to show that the drive you selected is now active.

Using DISKCOPY to Make Backups of the Quattro Pro Program Disks

Before you install Quattro Pro on your hard disk or run it from your floppy drive, you should make *backup copies* of the original program disks.

Obtain several blank 5.25" double-sided double-density disks or blank 3.5" double-sided double-density disks (set the same type as the original Quattro Pro disks). Because the DISKCOPY command copies the entire disk, you don't have to format the blank disks before you begin.

1. Change to the drive that contains the DOS program files.

2. If the DISKCOPY file is in a separate directory, change to that directory as explained earlier. For example, if the file is in the C:\DOS directory, type `cd\dos` at the C:> prompt, and press Enter.

3. Type `diskcopy a: a:` or `diskcopy b: b:`, depending on which drive you're using to make the copies.

4. Press Enter.

5. Follow the screen prompts to insert the source (original Quattro Pro) disk, then the target (blank) disk into the drive.

6. If you need to copy another original disk, press Y and go back to step 5. Continue until you copy all the original disks.

7. When you're done copying disks, type N when asked if you want to copy another disk.

8. Put the original disks back in their box and store them in a safe place.

Formatting Floppy Disks

The first step in preparing a floppy disk to store programs and data is formatting the disk.

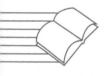

What is Formatting? The formatting procedure creates a map that later tells DOS where to find the information you store on the disk. You cannot place any information—programs or data of any kind—on a new disk before the disk is formatted. Formatting also erases any information on a diskette. *Do not* format your hard disk drive because formatting a hard disk erases all programs and information on the hard disk.

Use the following steps to format a disk:

1. Turn on your computer.

2. Change to the drive and directory that contains your DOS files. For example, if your DOS files are in C:\DOS, type cd\DOS at the C> prompt and press Enter.

3. Insert a blank disk into the A: or B: drive.

4. Type **FORMAT A:** or **FORMAT B:** and press Enter. The system will tell you to insert the disk (which you've already done).

5. Press Enter. The system then begins formatting the disk. When the format is complete, the system asks whether you want to format another.

6. Type **Y** if you want to format additional disks, then repeat all steps. Otherwise, type **N** to quit.

> **Labeling Disks** While the disk is being formatted, you can use the time to write the labels for the disks. Be sure to write on the labels before you attach them to the diskettes. (If you've already placed the labels on the diskettes, write on the labels using a felt-tip pen. The hard point of a ball-point pen can damage the surface of a diskette.)

Working with Directories

Because hard drives hold much more information than floppy drives, hard drives are usually divided into directories. For example, when you install Quattro Pro 3.0, the Installation program suggests that you copy the Quattro Pro program files to a directory called *QPRO* on drive C. This directory then branches off from the *root directory* of drive C, keeping all the Quattro Pro 3.0 program files separate from all other files on drive C. Directories can contain subdirectories as well.

Making Directories

To create a directory using the MD (Make Directory) command, use the following steps:

1. Change to the drive you want to create the directory on.

2. At the DOS prompt, type `md\`*`directoryname`*. (Substitute the name for the directory you are creating in place of *directoryname*.)

3. Press Enter. The directory now exists off the root directory. If you want to create a subdirectory off a directory, type the *directoryname*, a backslash and then a *subdirectoryname*, and press Enter.

You do not need to create a directory to run Quattro Pro; the installation program takes care of this for you. You may want to create additional directories to store your data files.

Moving to a Directory

To change directories with the CD (Change Directory) command, use the following steps:

1. Change to the drive that contains the directory.

2. At the DOS prompt, type `cd\`*`directoryname`*. (For example, type `cd\qpro`.) The backslash (\) you type tells DOS to begin at the root directory and move to the directory you specified under the root. Use the backslash to separate all directories and subdirectories in a command line. For example, to move to a subdirectory of a directory, the command line would look like this:

```
CD\directoryname\subdirectoryname
```

This command line specifies a complete *path* to the subdirectory.

3. Press Enter.

Displaying Directory Contents

To see which files are stored in a directory with the DIR (Directory) command, use the following steps:

1. Change to the drive and directory whose contents you want to view.

2. Type `dir` and press Enter. A list of files appears.

Working with Files

DOS also includes commands you can use to work with the files you create. This section briefly introduces the procedures for copying, deleting, and renaming files.

Copying Files

To copy files with the COPY command, use the following steps:

1. Move to the directory that stores the file (or files) you want to copy.

2. Type the command line:

```
COPY filename1 drive:\directoryname\filename2
```

In this command line, *filename1* is the name of the existing file you want to copy, *drive:\directoryname* is

149

the drive and directory you want to copy the file to, and *filename2* is the new name you want to give the copy of the file. If you want to create a copy of the file in the same drive or directory, you can omit the path (*drive:\directoryname*) before *filename2*.

3. Press Enter. DOS copies the file and places the copy in the current directory.

Deleting Files

To delete files with the DELETE (or DEL) command, use the following steps:

1. Move to the directory that stores the file you want to delete.

2. Type the command line:

   ```
   DEL filename
   ```

3. Press Enter.

4. When DOS asks you for confirmation, type **Y**. DOS deletes the file.

Renaming Files

To rename files with the RENAME (or REN) command, use the following steps:

1. Move to the directory that stores the file you want to rename.

2. Type the command line:

```
RENAME filename1 filename2
```

Or

```
REN filename1 filename2
```

In this command line, *filename1* is the name of the existing file, and *filename2* is the new name you want to assign to the file.

3. Press Enter. DOS renames the file and keeps it in the current directory.

For more information about using DOS commands, see *The First Book of MS-DOS.*

Index

153

D

X-Z

Count On Sams For All Your Spreadsheet Needs

The Best Book of Lotus 1-2-3, Release 3.1

Alan Simpson

This book is an in-depth, step-by-step tutorial covering all the features of 1-2-3 Release 3.1. You'll learn how to create 3-D worksheets, design and print graphs and reports, and desktop publish worksheets with the new WYSIWYG add-in.

750 pages, 7⅜ x 9¼, $27.95 USA
0-672-22713-4

The First Book of Lotus 1-2-3, Release 2.2

Alan Simpson & Paul Lichtman

This quick, practical guide is ideal for both the computer novice and the expert. It includes detailed coverage of the worksheet graphics and database management. QuickSteps provide simple keystroke sequences for specific tasks.

275 pages, 7⅜ x 9¼, $16.95 USA
0-672-27301-2

More Spreadsheet Titles From Sams

SAMS